CLASSIC COOKING

A New Approach to French Cuisine

CLASSIC COOKING

A New Approach to French Cuisine

by

JOHN MARSHALL

Castle Books, New York

Library of Congress Catalogue Card Number: 59-14826

First edition

This Edition Published By Arrangement
With Duell, Sloan & Pierce

FOR MY DAUGHTERS

MAYLIE *and* ANNE

CONTENTS

INTRODUCTION

In recent years fewer and fewer Americans have been content, as many were earlier, simply to eat what their parents ate. As Italian and Chinese restaurants spread across the country, even into its smaller cities, most Americans became aware of a wider world of food east and west. More and more Americans also traveled, and brought back with them, particularly those who had traveled in France, new standards of how fine food could be. And they and others became more venturesome at home in trying to achieve as high a standard in their own cookery.

In venturing this way myself I came to see how handicapped Americans are in this attempt to move into *haute cuisine*. It has its cookbooks, to be sure, but their directions tend to assume that one has learned to cook by cooking under expert guidance. Reading French readily, I have for years explored these professional French cookbooks, and believe I have now come to understand what their usually laconic directions imply. And having ferreted out their meaning, I became acutely aware of what they did not tell. This book attempts to tell it. Apart from its dedication to my daughters, who produced it by asking for it, this book is dedicated to people capable of learning what to do by reading.

It is, unashamedly, an elementary book for beginners in gourmetry. And who, unless he is standing still, is not beginning something? Possibly it even offers something for others already accomplished in cookery in various ways, possibly in helping them to make new starts on branches of good cookery they had not as yet explored or mastered.

A poet friend of mine, the late John Brooks Wheelwright, once remarked sagely that the qualities for which one initially disliked something often came to be the very qualities for which he came to value it. If initially the mass of words that follows seems great, remember that they are there because, in everything, this book starts from the beginning. It is for this reason that it is unashamedly more elementary, more rudimentary, than any cookbook I have encountered.

You can quickly test its efficacy for yourself. If, as a traveled gourmet, you asked yourself where in the world you would most like to have dinner tonight, the chances are that you would choose some favorite restaurant in France. If you and your guests could be miraculously transported there, your first concern would be to choose from its bill of fare what you most wanted to eat. If you were really wise in these premises, you would ask the maître d'hôtel to give you five or even ten minutes to read what was offered, as he gladly would. I'll wager that four times out of five you would eventually choose dishes this book will enable you to prepare for yourself. Test this contention for yourself by browsing in Parts II and III, "Thirty Menus" and "A la Carte," respectively, where the presentation is in fact in the form of a bill of fare.

For this is a book intended both to be read and to be used. Part I, "Good Cookery," is only to be read to reaffirm the standards by which good cookery yields good eating. Parts II and III are to be read to choose what you want to eat, and used to enable you to prepare it for yourself with a minimum of difficulty.

If initially you doubt your capability of preparing, four times out of five, as fine a meal as you would choose in any restaurant in the world, remember that you will be attempting it under optimum conditions. Obviously, there are some truly complicated dishes which only professional cooks, with all the resources that professional kitchens afford, can do. But the dishes you are likeliest to choose are most often relatively simple to prepare, almost too simple to be done well in a big kitchen where the cooks are under the pressure of orders from many patrons. Indeed, the real test of a big kitchen is whether or not it can produce these relatively simple dishes well for one, two, or at most four guests. You, on the other hand, will seldom cook for more.

Good cookery need not be too time-consuming if it is properly organized. In general, it falls into two distinct phases, the preparation of the ingredients, and the actual cooking. Usually you can prepare your ingredients pretty much at your convenience, as they are prepared by helpers in big kitchens. The actual cooking seldom requires more than thirty minutes, in some cases no more than fifteen. It is only in this second phase that timing becomes important, as you will see in the "Thirty Menus" of Part II.

Some aspirant cooks temperamentally resist the idea of cooking on time: they prefer, as they see it, to be creative in the kitchen. But creativity in the kitchen, as elsewhere in the arts, involves some uncertainty (which has no place in this one) as to how things are going to turn out. Thus creativity in the kitchen tends to be less constructive than in poetry or science. If you are still inclined toward it, at least once or twice submit yourself to the timing suggested in Part II and see if (1) the product is not better for it, and (2) you do not come to the table calmer and so better able to enjoy the better eating it affords.

Nor does this book demand more than minimum kitchen facilities and equipment such as the small apartment kitchens most of us cook in now can be made to afford. Its assumptions on this score are set forth in detail below, pp. 37 to 45. Restricted kitchen space is not a handicap, but rather an advantage in cooking for small numbers.

Though good eating was always an important consideration in my family, my education in *haute cuisine* began only in the Harvard Graduate School when I shared an apartment with the poets Robert Hillyer and Foster Damon. Tired of "eating around," as the phrase went in Cambridge, Damon, with his flair for research, decided that in a library as comprehensive as Widener there must somewhere be cookbooks, and duly found them there located logically in the stacks next to books on cremation. Though none of us had previous experience of good cookery, the books we found there proved the source of many an excellent meal.

Less adventurous than Damon, who has now collected cookbooks for years with notable results, I settled down on one now long out of print, but of which I eventually found a secondhand copy, *The Epicurean, A Complete Treatise of Analytical and Practical Studies on the Culinary Art . . . making a Franco-American Culinary Encyclopedia* by Charles Ranhofer, chef of Delmonico's, New York, Charles Ranhofer, Publisher, 1894, a work still used in better restaurant and club kitchens in the United States.

In the last ten years I have used and have come to prefer *L'Art Culinaire Français, Les Recettes de Cuisine, Pâtisserie, Conserves, des Maîtres contemporains les plus réputés, Ali-Bab, E. Darenne, E. Duval, A. Escoffier, Ph. Gilbert, B. Montaigné, Urban-Dubois, et al.,* published by Flammarion, Paris, 1950. This work is notable not only for its admirable choices of recipes, but as well for its photographs of basic procedures in the kitchen and its remarkable colored illustrations of how dishes should appear when best prepared and best presented. Two other more specialized sources have proved suggestive: *Les Poissons, Coquillages, Crustacés, leur Préparation culinaire*, by Michel Bouzy, Chef des Cuisines de la Maison Prunier, published in Paris, apparently by the author in 1929; and *Les Plaisirs de la Table*, by Edouard Nignon, published in Paris by the author, undated.

The contents of the present book have been tested for more than two years in an earlier, privately issued version entitled *Cooking on Time*. This earlier version was prepared at the request of my elder daughter on the occasion of her marriage, and has since been used by her wedding guests and others, to all of whom I am most grateful for much constructive criticism. In my elder daughter's constant use of it, it has passed its stiffest test: after having borrowed and used successfully my copy of *L'Art Culinaire Français* while I was in Europe, she asked that I bring her back a copy of it from France. On my return, I learned that it had just been published by Simon and Schuster of New York under the title, *The Art of French Cooking*, in what on examination proved to be an excellent translation, with the invaluable photographs and colored illustrations of the French original. If my elementary course in good cookery should lead others, as it did my daughter, to this fine work I should be amply rewarded.

Finally, I must acknowledge that apart from my reading I enjoyed for a happy interval being cooked for by Mrs. Magda Rasmussen Abraham, who had acquired the essentials of her art in Denmark and afterward became a *diplomée* of the Cordon Bleu in Paris. During these years I was privileged to suggest what was to be eaten and to watch its preparation at her skilled hands. (The Danish dessert of Menu 20, *Rød Grød*, is her recipe.)

This book probably had its inception in a remark of our dear and now long-dead Cambridge (Massachusetts) cook, Mittie, short for Mehitabel. Mittie was large, dark, and a wonderful cook in two senses: she was a natural cook, and she could read. From our tiny apartment kitchen she produced dinners of a quality and complication that astonished our guests. From such cookbooks as I then had

I imperfectly wrote out directions for her a day in advance. She studied them at home; but I always marveled, as her meals came to the table, how she managed them. One day I asked her how. "Why," she replied, "it isn't hard. When I get on the trolley to come out to Cambridge, I always think what I'll do first, what next, and then . . ." This, I submit, is one secret of true creativity in the kitchen.

J. M.

PART I

GOOD COOKERY

1. A QUALIFYING ROUND

Legend has it that an important medical-school examination once consisted of one sentence: "Write on milk." While milk plays an important role in cookery, as in physiology and psychiatry, the more appropriate question for a qualifying round in good cookery is "Write on eggs." In writing, briefly, on eggs, I can exemplify what this book is about, and you can come to an initial decision as to whether or not it is a book for you. Naturally, just as I suppose no physician's M.D. ever depended entirely on his response to one sentence, there is a great deal more in this book than there is in this one section of it. I have, for example, written much more fully on eggs, in Part III, pages 162 to 165: how to cook eggs in the various ways referred to briefly here is there given in detail.

But dealt with even briefly, eggs exemplify what are for this book the three first principles of good cookery: first, *have the best ingredients;* second, *cook them to bring out their best;* third, *minimize, or, better, avoid, the difficulties* in so cooking them, so that you may cook them, at their best, for yourself and your favored guests. The first two principles are standard for all good cookery; the third is not so generally recognized.

Eggs, in good cookery, usually involve only three basic ingredients: the eggs themselves, butter, and sometimes cream.

Fortunately good eggs, fresh eggs, are not hard to come by in the United States. The best source is some shop that specializes in eggs and dairy products, and thus, with a big turnover, has a constant fresh supply. Freshness, too, is easily determined: a truly fresh egg is one whose inner core of white (as contrasted with the always thinner outer core), when the egg is broken into a plate or pan, stands up around the yolk. If the eggs you are buying do not literally stand up to this test, try to find a better source of supply.

Finding good butter is, unfortunately, more of a problem. That canny New Englander, the late Professor George Lyman Kittredge, Shakespearean and Cape Codder, used to remark that there are three kinds of fish: fish that smells good, fish that doesn't smell, fish that smells bad. Butter that smells bad is a rarity; but so is butter that smells good—most butter doesn't smell. Undoubtedly its prevalence represents a considered policy on the part of butter producers: their aim is a product that displeases no one; if butter had a positive smell, it might displease someone. My solution of the problem is again to go to a shop that specializes in dairy products and there to buy not bar but tub butter. What I buy at the famous shop on Fulton Street goes there by the name of Omaha Sweet—it sweetens the ride uptown in the subway with its fragrance as it does the kitchen when it is melting on the stove.

To secure first-class cream presents no problem, with the fine, standardized American product what it is. And it is easy now to find homogenized sour cream, which is less expensive and preferable for most uses.

The second principle of good cookery, *how to bring out the best* in the ingredients, is particularly apt with respect to eggs. There are said to be niceties even in boiling them, as, for example, by cooking them in cold water gradually brought toward a boil, a procedure supposed to produce tenderer whites. Certainly, in regular boiling, one point is important, namely, putting the boiled egg immediately under cold water when the preferred boiling time in minutes has been attained, and for good reason: the egg has been cooked to the preferred time by intense heat from the outside; it continues to cook if the outside heat in its shell is not abruptly terminated.

Fried eggs by the American method of cooking them in a pan (the French have another—see page 200) vary greatly. You can fry them by frying bacon, and then simply dropping an egg into the hot bacon fat. The result may seem delicious if you (1) are on your honeymoon; (2) are in the woods; and (3) like eggs however they are cooked. A really well-cooked fried egg is a fresh egg that (1) is broken out of its shell with a minimum of disturbance so that its inner core of white stands up around the yolk; (2) is slipped into butter melted in a relatively cool frying pan; (3) is cooked in the butter so gently that it doesn't sizzle. For most tastes, in the finished product, the yolk should be firm on the outside and should run from the center when cut; the white should be shiny but tender from slow cooking. Similarly, shirred eggs are baked in an oven dish in butter in a slow oven so that their whites are mirror bright, as their French name, *oeufs au miroir*, implies they should be. And the same is true for what in the United States are called baked eggs: eggs broken into melted butter in individual custard cups, seasoned with salt and pepper, and topped with a tablespoonful of cream, preferably thick sour cream; to insure their slow baking they are cooked in a slow oven in an oven pan of water.

Of all the common ways of cooking eggs, scrambled eggs probably suffer most from unknowing cookery. The common mistake is to make them in a frying pan or even (as often in short-order restaurants) on the hot surface of a grill, so that the mixture toughens on contact with a broad, hot surface. The utensil to be used, rather, is a small sauce pan in which has been melted a first portion of butter: into it is poured the slightly beaten mixture of eggs, cream, salt and pepper, which is then slowly cooked with constant stirring; as it begins to thicken, its cooking is slowed down and its flavor enhanced by the addition of a second portion of butter. Scrambled eggs, so cooked, are soft, tender, small in curd, and really flavorsome.

The very term "dropped eggs" implies mishandling; "poached eggs," the preferable term, are gently broken into not boiling water, but water held just under a boil that has been salted and acidulated with a few drops of vinegar to help the whites to hold their shape. As in the case of fried eggs, for most tastes, poached eggs would be cooked only long enough for the yolks to be firm, but running from the center when cut.

Omelets suffer even more from inferior cookery. I had eaten first-class omelets in France, only lightly browned (if at all) on the outside, moist, but not fluffy through the middle. But in the earlier version of this book I had to acknowledge that I did not know how to achieve such a product. Shortly thereafter I *read* something that changed my life in the kitchen, a single sentence to the effect that after all a fine omelet is nothing more than scrambled eggs shaped and perhaps slightly browned. The consequence was the production of omelets that have won many compliments and may win them for you if you will follow the procedure given in detail in Part III, page 162.

The cookery of eggs exemplifies as well the third principle of all good cookery, *how to minimize or to avoid difficulties*. Most aspirant cooks have been led to believe that mayonnaise is difficult to make, and tricky because of a tendency to curdle. The truth is that anyone with an electric egg beater can make mayonnaise in five minutes or less with hardly any risk of curdling; if you turn the beater's crank yourself the same is true, except that it may take a little longer. The secret is to have the ingredients cold, and in hot weather to make the mayonnaise in an inner, smaller beating bowl set in a larger outside bowl with ice in it. You may well ask at this point, but why take the trouble, when you can so readily buy good mayonnaise? But the mayonnaise you buy is, like butter, made to displease no one. It supposedly consists of (1) egg yolks, (2) oil, (3) pepper, (4) salt, (5) mustard, (6) something acid such as vinegar or lemon juice. Among these six ingredients only two are standard, the salt and presumably the lemon juice. The others vary considerably. The combination of their variations, as you experiment with it, makes for a mayonnaise that sings for your palate. When once you have discovered your favorite combination of flavors, you will always prefer to make mayonnaise for yourself.

Have you been depriving yourself of the pleasures that hollandaise sauce provides because you have been told that it always curdles? You need deprive yourself and your guests of its pleasures no longer on that account if you will follow the simple procedure given for making it in Part III, page 155. Again the secret is using as little heat as possible in making what is essentially a warm mayonnaise, just as you make cold mayonnaise on ice, particularly in hot weather. By following the procedure given, I have not had a hollandaise curdle for more than ten years; and by this procedure it can be kept warm at least fifteen minutes, while the cook is enjoying his soup, for example. When you have mastered this sauce and its derivatives, e.g., *sauce béarnaise*, you are well on your way into *haute cuisine*, and without feeling any acute pain. Again, at this point, you may be asking, but why take the trouble? The answer is that a really well-made and well-flavored hollandaise sauce is the making of many a meal. For example, some evening when your appetite is finicky, buy some frozen asparagus spears on your way home. Steam rather than boil them for not more than twelve minutes, so that they are bright green and firm, not gray-green and mushy. While they are steaming make some hollandaise and toast some bread and give yourself the pleasure of asparagus on toast, hollandaise. From that night on you will make hollandaise—and all the more in the spring when fresh asparagus at moderate prices is on the market.

Some of the other egg sauces are admittedly complicated and even tricky, or seem so the first time you make them, as, for example, the *sauce vin blanc* for sole Marguéry of Menu 29. But if you will follow the procedure for making it which that menu offers, you will be minimizing and avoiding the difficulties that might otherwise confront you. It might amuse you even now to compare the detailed directions given there with a famous recipe for this classic dish:

> Cook in *fumet de poisson* filets of sole laid flat. Surround them with mussels poached in white wine, and shrimps. Cover with white wine sauce. Glaze quickly under the broiler.

There is, of course, a great deal more of good cookery with respect to eggs, as the section devoted to them in Part III indicates (see pages 162 to 165). This brief treatment of it is given here, as was suggested at the outset, not for your guidance, but merely to exemplify the principles of all good cookery, *ab ovo*.

2. BUYING

To buy the best ingredients need be no chore, but, at its best, a weekly expedition into the market district of your city, a weekly expedition that I have for years looked forward to on Saturday mornings. I suppose every city has some kind of market district. In Boston, it was around Faneuil Hall; in New York it is around the now-abandoned Washington Market that was my Saturday-morning haunt; in Geneva . . . Somewhere in your city is a market district, with retail shops, for meat, vegetables, butter, eggs, and cheese, and some other shops that specialize in special groceries. Going there once a week provides you not only with the best ingredients, but with your best ideas about what you would like to eat. Ideally, a cook should always do his own shopping. He becomes, from the experience of cooking, the best judge of what ingredient is best. But it is also in shopping that he sees what he would like to cook.

On a typical Saturday morning in New York, I take the Broadway local from Christopher Street to Cortlandt Street, with a general idea of what I want to buy. "A general idea" means a basic list: butter, cheese, crab, two meats, salad, fruit. I go first to the famous shop on Fulton Street and say "a pound of Omaha Sweet," or even "two pounds," and have my butter. Then I consult with the men who own the shop about what cheeses we might most enjoy; and, taking their advice, go off with a pound or so. I then stop at another shop, and discuss meats; if I have Menu 2 in mind, I go to the shop that has especially good pork chops; if I want a calf's foot, to the shop where they surely can be found. I then wander on to a particularly congenial fish shop, where, apart from being able to find the best of all available fish, in the small restaurant now incorporated with it I can have a cup of coffee, or a glass of beer, or, if my need is exigent, six beautiful and freshly opened oysters with a bottle of stout! Over them the sea food for the weekend is decided on. At this point I subside briefly into the subway, refreshed by the smell (positive) of my Omaha Sweet.

Inevitably, anyone cannot always afford the time for such a weekly expedition into the market district. Against this contingency, or that of not having a market district handy, there are other possibilities. Good cookery for the best ingredients usually requires four good shops: as remarked, one specializing in "dairy" products, eggs, cheese, and butter; a good shop for fish; a good butcher; a good shop for vegetables. In addition, it is useful to have your eye on a shop that specializes in special groceries, Italian, Greek, Turkish, or Indian. In a city such as New York such shops exist in almost every quarter, if you seek them out.

In New York, or elsewhere, my general rule would be to look for the shops that look old. In suburbia somewhere or other there will surely be an old "butter and eggs" shop: the chances are that the owner is hoping, against stiff competition, to survive by having a better product; if so, he is your man. "Good" shops for fish and meat tend also to be the older shops: typically, they are shops with sawdust on the floor, tended by men in white butchers' aprons, and possibly even wearing a straw hat during the winter; very little fish or meat is shown; it is all well stowed away under proper refrigeration; but ask, and you shall be given. Furthermore, these white-aproned proprietors—for they usually are that—are the instructors who can and will tell you how to buy fish or meat. If I am *instruit*, as the French say, in either regard, I must here bow briefly to Vincent Petrosino and Harry Lipps, who for me will continue to represent fish and meat of the old Washington Market. As for a good shop for vegetables, it is more and more likely to be found in your immediate neighborhood: greengrocers are seemingly a coming breed in the United States. To choose yours in the neighborhood there are three easy tests: Are the salad greens well arranged and regularly sprinkled? Are the mushrooms white and firm (they can hardly be in hot weather, so that this is a severe test)? What is the attitude to your fingering the fruit (this is the stiffest test, because if they see that you do it gently, and in the interest of finding just what you want, they will not object)?

In any case, you will do well to begin and learn from such shops. After you have learned, it may well be that you can pick up bargains elsewhere including the "chain stores," which, with their enormous purchasing power, often, but not always, offer real bargains. A warning: do not avoid a shop that seems to you always too full of clients; it may be full because it is known to the neighborhood as its best shop. If you can impress your identity on one clerk, you will discover that you can telephone him in advance, and have him set aside the best of what you want till you come in for it; mistakenly I avoided for several years what I now know to be the best source in my neighborhood of veal scaloppine on Bleecker Street because it was always too full—and for good reason.

That shop that deals in special groceries. . . . Almost every neighborhood now has somewhere an Italian grocery to which you should make an expedition for Menu 9; you will see there more things you want to eat than the menu calls for; go at your own peril. For Indian, that is, East Indian, comestibles you may have to look further: the shop where you find them may be rather fancy in its way, because it has British products, or products which, after the Anglo-Indian period, are regarded as British: the best curries, chutney, etc. It may, for example, be a shop, like the famous one in Paris just back of the Madeleine, which prides itself on having anything which comes from overseas. But almost any American city has such shops somewhere.

Having dwelt on the principles of good cookery, two that are general to all discussion of the subject, *having the best ingredients*, and *cooking them to bring out their best*, but not yet having explained how you may *minimize or, better, avoid the difficulties* in cooking them so, may I venture a fourth principle, which will be implicit, and occasionally explicit, in what follows—*have fun:* shopping can be fun.

3. THE CARE AND PRESERVATION OF...

Quite as important as the buying of first-class ingredients is the care you give them while they are in the house before you are ready to use them.

Some foods, most notably fish, can hardly be kept without deterioration for any length of time. With fish, buy it and cook it is the best rule. Catch it and cook it is still better; but few can, save on their vacations. The fish you buy usually seems better if thoroughly washed under running cold water and dried with paper towels. Aside from that the best you can hope is that it was really fresh when you bought it.

Most meats keep well, some very well, under electric refrigeration, if properly handled. The best method of keeping meat I learned from my trusty butcher, Harry Lipps of the famous firm, E. Joseph and Sons, formerly in the Washington Market. Each Thursday he takes home his week's supply of meat, and choice I am sure that it is. Each lot he unwraps from its market papers and rewraps in aluminum foil. It is thus kept as cold as refrigeration will keep it, the foil transmitting the cold and not insulating the meat from it as paper does and preventing the drying that electric refrigeration causes.

The tenderer vegetables require similar care. First-class mushrooms will remain first class for some days if placed unwashed in an airtight plastic box under refrigeration. Carrots last well if kept in the refrigerator in the plastic bags in which they are now often sold. If you are fortunate in having a closed, refrigerated vegetable bin, virtually all vegetables (save those you want to ripen, e.g., tomatoes, which generally seem better for two or three days in the sun on a window sill) stay in better condition there, most of all the tenderer greens, salad greens, parsley, etc. Of course one rotting vegetable can contaminate the entire bin, and its contents should be checked frequently to detect any rot early. If it occurs, the bin itself should be thoroughly washed with some mild detergent, and the unrotted vegetables should be well washed under running water. To minimize the risk (and to save space) it is well, in the case of lettuce, for example, to remove the outside leaves you are unlikely to be using and to wash the remaining head under running water before it goes into the bin. Washing parsley and water cress before they go in is similarly advantageous, both for cleanliness and for keeping them fresh. If you are not fortunate in having such a bin, a covered enamel refrigerator box on a shelf serves the same purposes quite as well.

A really good cook is also much concerned with preserving sauces he has prepared for later use and the leftovers from what he has cooked. Sauces, prepared or leftover, stay good for surprising lengths of time in pint or smaller screw-top jars, if the jars are made relatively sterile by rinsing them with hot water, and the sauce is poured into them immediately after reheating to a boil. Any sauce that develops a mold, or is in any way suspicious, should, of course, be discarded at once, for their broths are an ideal culture for the development of harmful bacteria. Leftover meats again are best preserved in aluminum foil, and for the same reason as for meats that are uncooked.

Most cheeses, except for some of the harder varieties, should not be refrigerated after you have bought them. Indeed, it is now recognized to be unfortunate that they have to be refrigerated at all, as they undoubtedly have to be in modern mass distribution. For the creamier cheeses, such as camembert or brie, the blue cheeses, and even the hard cheeses such as cheddar and Muenster, the best rule is to buy several days in advance only as much as you can readily use, and to allow them to ripen outside the refrigerator before you serve them. The blue cheeses can be kept in prime condition for some time in a closed jar made for the purpose with corrugations on its bottom, between which is poured a mixture of vinegar and salt. The soft whole-milk and cream cheeses, of course, require constant refrigeration.

Prime fruit can be kept static in its ripening in the vegetable bin and then brought to perfect ripeness in a sunny window. It is good practice to buy melons some days before you want to use them, to watch their final ripening for yourself. And the same applies to the salad fruit, alligator pears or avocados.

The preservation of foods and leftovers ought to be the concern of the cook himself, both to keep the contents of the refrigerator in constant use, and thus avoid spoiling, and for what they may suggest to him. Often something there suggests an entire meal. Or, again, when he is preparing a meal for himself alone, it may suggest some interesting experiment that will later flower for his guests. Good food, even when left over, can breed other good meals.

A really good cook has three salient personal characteristics. (1) He is never entirely satisfied with the way he has cooked a given dish, and is, while eating it, making mental notes as to how he could make it better the next time. (2) Before he gets up from the table at any meal, he is thinking, if he has not already decided, of what the next one will be. (3) He is convinced, and tends to convince others, that no matter how tenuous his appetite (or theirs) he can think of something that would taste good. And these three important characteristics are nourished and developed as he contemplates in the kitchen what he has on hand and what there is left over.

4. COOKING WITH HEAT

Good cookery, in bringing the best ingredients to their best, is largely a matter of *how to heat* and of *how to build in flavor*. This section will deal briefly, and in terms of general principles, with the recurrent and fundamental ways of heating.

Even *boiling* has its small but essential niceties. If something, e.g., a vegetable, is being boiled to serve, the boiling should be as brief as is required to yield the tenderness you want. The process should not be started until the water is boiling furiously, over heat sufficient, if possible, to keep the ingredient at a boil all the time it is in the water. Today, brevity of boiling is far more generally recognized than in the earlier days of soggy cabbage and gray peas. After all, few vegetables need more than fifteen minutes to be tender, and many not more than five, e.g., cabbage and spinach. Unless for some reason you want the water to boil away as the ingredient is done, an ample quantity of water is to be preferred, because its volume makes it easier to keep it at a boil as the cold ingredient goes in. In the end, except for this consideration, the amount makes little difference, if you finish the job in the French way, by pouring off the water, by setting the pan and its drained contents back on the heat to dry, and by melting in it the butter you usually wish to add before serving.

For some vegetables, particularly asparagus, broccoli, fine new potatoes, and squash, *steaming* is to be preferred. The times required are about the same in a tightly covered steamer; and the product, in the case of asparagus and broccoli, hasn't been damaged by bumping about in boiling water; or, in the case of squash, is less watery.

If, on the other hand, you are *boiling* something to extract its flavor, as for soups or sauces, the process is reversed. You put the ingredient into the water cold, and bring it slowly to a boil, continue to simmer it for some time; in general, the longer the better. Ingredients so cooked should be, and are, useless in themselves, for in such cooking all their flavor and some of their fiber should be extracted. Don't be surprised if your cat or even your dog turns up his nose at them. It's not wasteful to throw them away, as you should: they have served their purpose in what they gave up.

Frying is generally supposed to be more of an art than it really is. The secret of it is concealed in a recurrent phrase in French cookbooks: "Fry till properly brown and then set in a warm place." In good cookery, relatively few ingredients are finished in the frying pan on top of the stove. They are simply *first* cooked there, usually at a brisk heat which (1) seals the outside to conserve the inside juices, and (2) gives them much the appearance you want when they appear on the table. Their cooking *through* occurs in a "warm place," in real practical English, in a warm oven. The "frying" of the thin veal slices known as scaloppine of Menus 4 and 26 consists of exposing them only most briefly to heat in the frying pan on the top of the stove, and then finishing them in a warm oven. But this frying exemplifies another important consideration in this method of heating—the glaze. As noted in the detailed directions of these two menus, as the juices of the veal mingle with the fat in the pan, they begin to form a brown coating on the pan's bottom. This is not to be avoided as some might think, but rather to be encouraged for two reasons: first, as in these menus it can be utilized to give the veal slices a golden brown simply by rubbing them gently in it during their quick top-of-the-stove cooking, and second, because this "glaze" becomes the basis of their eventual sauce.

As for the fat essential to this *first stage of frying*, butter is definitely to be preferred. It is here that its fine flavor is built in in both the meat and the glaze. True, it has a tendency to burn quickly. But if there is any special art in frying, it is at this stage, in seeing that the frying goes neither too slow nor too fast. The control is simple; it need not involve tinkering with the heat; rather, by holding the handle of the frying pan in your left hand and your two-tined frying fork in your right hand, you can slow the process by lifting the pan from the heat, or accelerate it by restoring it to the heat.

Usually the *second stage of frying* involves (1) the slow cooking through of the sealed meat in a warm oven, and (2) the making of its sauce in the frying pan on the top of the stove. The only attention required for the first or oven phase is to be sure that the oven does not become more than warm, certainly not more than 300°, often less. The other phase, making the sauce, occupies you only briefly:

first you put into the glazed pan over low heat the ingredients that give the sauce its added flavors, e.g., chopped shallots (or onions), perhaps mushroom slices, and allow them to fry gently in the remaining grease, to bring them to full flavor, very probably salting at this point to persuade the mushroom slices to yield their juice under the influence of salt. As they yield it, you begin the "deglazing" of the frying pan by loosening the glaze in the spreading mushroom juice with a wooden spoon. You complete the deglazing at about this point by adding some liquid, usually a meat stock (consommé) or white or red wine. The process of deglazing is repeated in this new liquid, again by loosening it and stirring it in with a wooden spoon. The sauce is then left simmering, usually until some final thickening, while the meat continues cooking through in the warm oven. Also, as a final touch, any juices that develop in the oven are poured into the sauce. Frying by this method gives you meats that are properly browned or gilded outside, tender and juicy inside, *and* a sauce that epitomizes the full flavor of the process. Furthermore, such frying need not be hectic: the one tricky part, the initial sealing, is accomplished well ahead of time. And if you have properly utilized the precious glaze on the frying pan, it will be virtually clean when you have finished with it.

This process is essentially the same for all meats, e.g., the chicken Bercy of Menu 1, the pork chops of Menu 2. With vegetables, e.g., mushrooms, they are often finished in the pan on the top of the stove (see p. 170).

To return for a moment to the question of frying fat: as I have said, butter is definitely to be preferred. Margarine I find hopeless in flavor and behavior. The vegetable fats, if you can't bring yourself to use butter, are amenable: they don't burn; they have no flavor that is objectionable; their deficiency is in their lack of the positive and agreeable flavor that good butter contributes. Oil, vegetable or olive, is all very well if you like its flavor in frying and can readily digest things fried in it. A half-and-half mixture of butter and oil has the advantage that the butter doesn't brown so rapidly and still imparts its flavor. Oil certainly has its place in another kind of frying, deep-fat or French frying, but in this book this kind of frying is dealt with at the end as a kind of postgraduate course (see pp. 198 to 204).

My remarks on *broiling* will apply only to the two meats which are best cooked in this way, beef and lamb. Perhaps chicken should be included, but I happen to like it less well when it is broiled. For beef and lamb steaks or chops, broiling is definitely the preferred treatment. Again, as in frying, the quick sealing of the meat on the outside is essential. To facilitate it, (1) rub vegetable or olive oil vigorously into the meat, together with salt and pepper; (2) broil it in a preheated broiler, as close to the heat as you can manage without setting fire to the accumulating fat in the pan. I might as well confess that for me a well-done piece of beef is spoiled. And against most American tastes, but in strict accord with French taste, this goes for lamb as well as for beef. Not that I like these meats raw: for me the ideal product should be dark brown on the outside, on the verge of being burned, with the inside rapidly graduating through darkening pinks to red but thoroughly warmed meat at the center. To assure such a product, your steaks or chops should be thick, at least an inch and a half for beefsteaks, at least an inch thick for lamb chops. For such a steak, set the Minute Minder (see p. 38) at fifteen minutes as the steak goes into the preheated broiler. Give each side three minutes of the broiler's top heat, then each side two. At five minutes on the Minute Minder (i.e., after this total of ten minutes' broiling) turn off the broiler heat and leave the steak in the hot broiler; this is known as allowing it to "rest." Actually it is receiving its final cooking; essentially, broiling is cooking by quick heat from the outside; when the source of that heat is turned off, the heat that is still outside in the broiler continues to penetrate, but more gently; and thus this heat slowly graduates the brusque transition from a steak that is well cooked on the outside and raw in the middle to a steak that is evenly cooked through.

For lamb chops, the procedure is the same, except that for inch-thick chops the total cooking time need be no longer than ten minutes. If you can overcome any prejudice you may feel against pink lamb, and will try chops once that way, you will never again revert to the grayish, overcooked product that usually appears on American platters.

Broiling is invariably finished by the addition of butter. If you prefer the butter melted and mixed with the meat juices, you may add it to the meat as the resting period begins. But the French procedure seems preferable: the butter, mixed with finely chopped parsley, and, if you will and can, such other fresh herbs as tarragon or thyme, is laid cold on the steak or chops as they go to the table, so that any melting that occurs takes place under your or your guests' greedy eyes.

While speaking of broiling, possibly we should speak briefly of other uses of the broiler. They occur in giving the final touch to dishes that are not and could not be broiled, e.g., a fine cheese omelet with a bit of grated cheese on top, or the celery Mornay of Menu 30, which requires for its final touch the tiny spots of brown that characterize sauce Mornay at its best. In such instances you put the dish in question under the preheated broiler, as close to its heat as you dare, for a few dedicated seconds, during which you do nothing except watch for it to acquire from this quickest of all available heats in the contemporary kitchen just the brown, or touches of brown, you wish it to have.

Though our French friends of the kitchen have a saying which they constantly reiterate, to the effect that roast cooks are born and not made, I see nothing very esoteric about good roasting, possibly because we can control its temperatures rather better than when meats were roasted on spits in front of a fire, or in ovens with variable heat. But good *roasting* does depend on two related considerations, the first of which is that no, but no, moisture is added. By adding no moisture, the principal variables become the roasting time and the temperature. There are different schools of thought on this subject, but most agree that the oven should be hot when a roast goes into it; the differences relate as to how hot. Again the principle is the same: sealing the outside of the meat to conserve its inner juices. The French cooking times are as follows, though remember that the French like their red meats rare:

Roast beef: from 12 to 15 minutes per pound.
Roast veal: 30 minutes per pound.
Leg of lamb: 15 minutes per pound.
Roast pork: 30 minutes per pound.
Baked ham: from 20 to 25 minutes per pound.
Roast chicken: from 13 to 15 minutes per pound, or better, 40 minutes for an average small chicken, 50 minutes for the same bird stuffed.
Roast duck: 15 minutes per pound, unstuffed.

Roast turkey: 15 to 20 minutes per pound (stuffed or unstuffed, respectively).

These times work well at an average oven heat of 350°, which may be raised to 400° at the end to produce the brown that you want.

Of the two considerations on which good roasting depends, the first, never, but never add moisture, may seem radical only with respect to poultry. For poultry, rather than adding moisture, one should add grease, and in its uncooked skin. Three minutes, or better five, devoted to rubbing softened butter into the skin of a chicken or turkey will bring literally rich returns. Duck and geese have the grease they need for roasting evenly distributed under their skin (to keep them warm in the water which is their habitat): they roast well in their own grease, with none added, and eventually most of theirs poured off (see Menu 27). The other meats, veal, lamb, pork, and beef, usually have sufficient fat outside to need none added, unless the cut in question is utterly lean. Thus if you ever roast a beef tenderloin, as well you might, it will be better roasted if larded (see Menus 28 and 29); that is, pierced with small strips of fat, preferably beef fat rather than pork.

Not adding moisture to a roast leads to the second consideration in good roasting: making the sauce. Without moisture, the juices of the roasting meat "fall to a glaze" on the bottom of the pan. When a roast is done, set it in a "warm place," again a warm oven, preferably on the platter on which it is to be served, to rest like a steak and thereby to even out its cooking; pour off any fat in the pan, and "deglaze" it, precisely as in frying, with meat stock or wine. Unthickened, the product becomes the juice of roast beef—"au jus"; or thickened, the natural sauce for the meat in question: in either case a sauce that epitomizes its flavor.

The last way of heating, the most effective for building in flavor, and probably the least used in the United States, is *braising*. It is defined in *L'Art Culinaire* as "the most costly and the hardest to succeed with." It need be neither. Essentially, braising is slow simmering in a highly flavored broth, best exemplified in the braising of a ham as in Menu 30. First, it is left to absorb the flavors of the process cold for as many as twelve hours, in (1) wine, in this case sherry; (2) vegetables, in this case carrots, onions, and celery; (3) herbs, in this case parsley, thyme, and marjoram; (4) in spices, in this case cloves and pepper. These seasonings are then fried together, strained off from the wine, to bring them, particularly the vegetables, to full composite flavor. The ham is then returned to them with the now seasoned wine and diluted meat stock (consommé) and cooked in this liquid slowly on the top of the stove, or more easily in a slow oven for three hours. The ham is then removed from the reduced liquid and it is further reduced, with as much as possible of the fat eliminated by skimming while it boils, and, clarified and thickened slightly, it becomes the sauce for the braised ham, which likewise epitomizes all its and the added flavors. In principle, all meats may be braised, as are the sweetbreads of Menu 28 and the beef short ribs of Menu 29 in this book, with slight differences.

And so may certain vegetables, most notably endives, celery, and onions, though with them the process need not be so complicated: braising, for them, means still a slow simmering in a well-buttered baking dish in a rich stock, with the stock reduced as a glaze for them rather than as a sauce. (See Menu 14.)

These are the principal and recurrent ways of cooking with heat. We'll now turn briefly to other methods of preparing food which are equally an integral part of good cookery.

5. COLD COOKERY

To cook is a verb deriving in English, French, and German from the Latin *coquere.* From its origins it has been associated but not necessarily confined to cooking with heat. More essentially, it means preparing for the table food that is eaten there, just as the related word kitchen (cuisine) is the place where food is so prepared. Some dishes are intended to arrive at the table cold, even chilled, and are at their best so. The process of preparing them belongs equally to good cookery.

The most relevant forms of cold cookery in the present context are the meat jellies, or aspics, which are essentially meat sauces or broths, and which from their own or added gelatin turn to jelly when chilled. In general, they represent a component of the classic bill of fare that tends to be neglected in the United States. They develop almost of themselves when certain dishes are chilled and served cold, as in the variant beef à la mode of Menu 29, or the braised ham of Menu 30. But aspic is a most agreeable sauce for other ingredients, most notably the meat pastes, and most notably of all of the king of them, *pâté de foie gras.*

In such uses it is essentially a basic sauce and as such is more readily prepared and utilized than most aspirant cooks imagine. Thus in Menu 24 and in Part III (pp. 177 to 179) the procedure is given for making individual aspics of *pâté de foie gras* which, apart from being easy, and relatively inexpensive, requires no longer than thirty minutes. In cold cookery, the use of aspic (meat or other jellies) is fundamentally intended first to add flavor, as in a sauce, and second, and quite as importantly, to conserve the flavor and moisture of whatever is the inner component. Thus salmon, cold, is much the better for a coating of fish aspic applied first when it is still moist from its original cooking with heat. (See p. 182.)

There is, of course, similar cold cookery with respect to soups (the jellied consommés and cold cream soups such as vichyssoise and cold cream of curry. See pp. 148 and 149, respectively) and with respect to desserts, such as the ices, and in this book Turinois of Menu 27 and the mousse of chocolate of Menu 30.

But the major form of cold cookery here and on most American tables resides in salads. In their simplest and most preferable form the cookery involved is in the preparation of the appropriate sauce for the ingredient or ingredients in question. The range of salads is dealt with in Part III (pp. 172 to 176), and this is the place for only some general remarks on general principles.

Returning to basic principles, the first is, as always, having the best ingredients both for the salad itself and for its sauce (dressing).

For the ingredients, the supply has improved enormously in recent years, at least in metropolitan shops. Even a few years ago it was hard to find anything but the abominable iceberg lettuce, cabbagey and not fit for any truly self-respecting table. Now any proper vegetable shop offers as well (or better) Boston, or native lettuce, romaine, chicory, escarole, water cress, endive, and in the autumn and winter months field salad (the French *Mâche*). More recently still in New York shops has appeared the fine Bibb lettuce, formerly obtainable only in the states near to its state of origin, Kentucky, with its rich green leaves and unusually succulent stem portions.

A green salad made of one or at most two of these ingredients is good enough for anyone, and better than one made of more. The current vogue for a "tossed" salad is a diversion from good taste: any green salad is tossed or thoroughly mixed into its accompanying sauce, even "labored," as the French say, who prefer theirs worked into its sauce until the greens are somewhat wilted by its vinegar; but to make a tossed salad of many ingredients, particularly when sliced green peppers are included, is so to confound its flavor as to leave only something that is noxious and indigestible. (I confess to being allergic to green peppers; a lot of people are, but they don't know it.) Most Americans prefer, and rightly, a green salad in which the greens are still green and a bit crisp. To achieve it, it should be tossed or labored just before serving, enough so that each dry leaf is thoroughly coated by, but not wilted by, the sauce.

As to the sauce or dressing, the supply of essential ingredients is also much improved. They are oil, some acid, salt, pepper, possibly mustard, and always, for me, garlic. Good oils, preferably, of course, olive oils, are now more readily available on the American market than ever before, and at lower prices. The finest olive oils continue to be French, but they are consequently still the most expensive. Try a variety of Italian, Spanish, and Greek olive oils in that order till you find one that sings for you, and then buy a gallon of it: bottle it off in quart bottles and put them in the darkest, coolest closet that you have, and you will have the fine olive oil that you want for a variety of uses at minimum expense. The acids, vinegars, are now readily available in a wide range of bases and flavors. There are, for example, vinegars based on cider, wine, and malt, pure, or flavored with tarragon, dill, and other herbs. With salt, pepper, and garlic remaining relatively standard (except that pepper should always be freshly ground, particularly for salad, from whole peppercorns) there is a variety of mustards. Thus you can vary your basic salad dressings, by varying their ingredients, from day to day.

And then you may vary your salads by moving into salads of other kinds, the so-called *salades composées*, of which most Americans know only one, Waldorf salad, made with sliced celery, sliced apples, and chopped walnuts blended in mayonnaise. There are others, as Menu 24 will tell you. Furthermore, their preparation involves building in flavor cold, as the procedure for preparing this particular salad, Belle Hortense, will indicate: you are to prepare it the previous day so that the celery which is its central ingredient may absorb the flavor of its sauce, sauce rémoulade.

About salads one final word. For reasons that escape me salads in the United States have come to be associated with wood, with wooden bowls, with wooden salad spoons and forks. No matter how these wooden implements are washed, sooner or later they accumulate flavor, and a flavor that is increasingly undesirable—rancid, to put it bluntly. We wondered for some time what had gone wrong with our salads: it was the wooden bowl. Why not follow the French, and serve your salads in glass bowls, with silver spoons and forks?

6. BUILT-IN FLAVOR

The process of *building in flavor* has already been exemplified in the classic procedure for braising a ham (p. 128). It is so basic to good cookery, however, that it deserves a somewhat more detailed treatment.

The sources of flavor in classic good cookery are in general those of braising: *wine* (occasionally spirits), *vegetables, herbs, and spices.* And, for full flavor, these components figure in cooking recurrently. Thus, as in braising a ham, it is first soaked (or marinated) in them cold, then cooked in them, with the vegetables previously fried to bring them to their full flavor; then served in a sauce composed of them, reduced in volume to bring them to their peak. Actually, they figure in the process a fourth time, in the consommé which was added as the cooking began; for the beef from which the consommé was made had been seasoned in the making with all of them save wine.

Good cookery certainly involves knowing when *not* to build in flavor. Often the less flavor added to the very best ingredients the better. An absolutely fresh sole as fine as the Dover sole of the English Channel is undoubtedly at its best when simply fried lightly in the best butter, or even lightly broiled, served, perhaps, with more butter, parsley, and a wedge of lemon for those who like a dash of its juice. A first-class steak is similarly at its best when simply rubbed with oil, broiled, and served with parsley butter. A delicate cream soup, such as cream of chestnuts, wants no flavor but its own. Really fresh lobster deserves simply to be boiled and eaten warm with melted butter or cold with fine mayonnaise.

On the other hand, other ingredients, even at their best, benefit from judiciously added flavor. The best lamb chop, to my taste, improves from having been lightly rubbed with garlic before broiling, so lightly that one can hardly detect its addition. Pork chops benefit from a touch of thyme. Spinach is more palatable for some if slightly flavored with nutmeg, though the spice is noxious to others.

In the end, there are relatively few dishes which do not benefit from some added flavor, and this gradual building in of them is one of the most striking differences between good cookery and ordinary cookery, where all too often the cook believes his work to be finished by adding some seasoning as his final touch.

Thus a good cook does not begrudge the time he invests in preparing the sources of these flavors which are, in general, three in number: *stocks, basic sauces*, and one for which I know no English name, *mirepoix*, and which happens to figure only once in this book, in the soup, cream of shrimp (see p. 146), and so may be passed over rapidly: it represents a variety of the flavoring vegetables, finely chopped and as always fried to bring them to full flavor, but used without moistening.

For purposes of this book the preparation of two of the basic stocks, those of beef and chicken, requires no more time than that of opening a can; for, some of my purist friends to the contrary, the fine beef and chicken consommés now readily available in cans seem to me to serve as well and probably better than stocks of those meats that one prepares for himself. I say this, though I confess to enjoying their preparation and often indulge in the fun of it. But it is at best a rather messy and protracted business: beef stock, for example, requires a minimum of eight hours' simmering; and to achieve a fine product requires clarification with lightly beaten whites of eggs and straining through cloths. Unfortunately, no canner has yet produced a third stock, that of veal, which is much called for in French cookery; it is therefore not specified in this book; I occasionally invest eight hours in it, and usually reduce it to a thick jelly, to produce an allowable final seasoning for meat sauces, *veal glaze*. The fourth stock, of fish (*fumet de poisson*), is easily and quickly made, and it appears, with directions for making it, in Menu 25, as the basis for the white wine sauce of sole Marguéry.

These stocks, with their built-in flavor, are most frequently used in the basic sauces, particularly in three of them, brown sauce, clear brown sauce, and the velvets (*veloutés*), the preparation of which is described in detail on pp. 151 to 154. The fourth, white sauce (*béchamel*), derives from a stock of another base, milk, but again milk flavored with much the same ingredients (see p. 154). The building in of the flavors of these basic sauces has already been once exemplified, in the description of Veal Chasseur, and they figure repeatedly in this book in this role.

Other sauces, usually served apart from the dish in question, give each individual the privilege of building in some final, usually contrasting, flavor for himself. Of these two have already been mentioned in this role, mayonnaise and hollandaise. In fact, flavor at its best seems to reside in two basic considerations, compatibility and contrast, best dealt with, as it is in the following pages, in terms of menu making and serving.

7. MENU MAKING

Certainly menu making should be an integral part of good cookery, and it should belong to the cook as much as shopping. For he is best qualified, within the general wishes and tastes of his guests, to decide what the menu of a given day is best made up of, in terms of what is on the market, what his time allows in terms of preparations and actual cooking, and, finally, in some measure, in terms of what he would enjoy cooking.

Within these terms the cook thinks first, like a traveled gourmet confronted with a restaurant bill of fare, of what the main dish is to be: all else, in varying degrees, relates to it. What is to accompany it, what precedes, and what follows—and, in addition, what wine or wines. In such thinking rule the two considerations just mentioned: compatibility and contrast.

Of the two, contrast is less often in play. In the menus of this book, as I review them, it is seldom violent, as, for example, in one combination very much to my liking, cold sliced white meat of turkey and the hottest prepared mustard. Others like the sharpness of various pickles with dishes that are generally bland. Contrast, for me, is at its best in contrasts between rather than within courses: probably most would agree in not wanting a cream soup before a main dish with a sauce based on cream, whereas a relatively sharp consommé, further sharpened with a slice of lemon, would go well. Most Americans would draw back from a fish and meat in the same course, though the French are less timid of this particular contrast, and often garnish steaks, for example, with the ultra-fishiness of anchovies. On the other hand, this is a contrast to which Americans do not object in *hors d'oeuvres variés*, where they tend to eat the fish and meat components at the same time, whereas Europeans tend to eat the fish components first (in the order of the classic menu) and the meat components later. It is with these considerations in mind that I have suggested anchovies on toast as a preliminary to the steak dinner of

Menu 12. Of the two considerations, compatibility and contrast, I suspect that compatibility, with such exceptions as those noted, overrules. This would be the case, for example, with the Italian meal, Menu 9, with the sharpness of an antipasto in its preliminary course, the sturdiness of spaghetti with its rich tomato sauce for the main dish, with its sharper spaghetti cheese, and the blandness of Italian cottage cheese, ricotta, sweetened or spiced for its sequel: here are relatively gentle contrasts between courses, which (usually with the additions of other courses) have proved their compatibility in Italian taste.

Of course tastes in compatibility vary greatly. I no longer agree to the maxim of my New England boyhood that

> Pie without cheese,
> Is like a kiss without a squeeze.

But I seldom now eat pie (for reasons that will appear), and the cheeses I most enjoy are not particularly compatible with pie. Possibly you, too, prefer your favorite cheeses now with some relatively unobtrusive water biscuit that contrasts with but does not overpower it. Or you may, like many Americans, prefer to eat your cheeses without bread or crackers, as a contrast to the sharpness of a fine green salad.

In the menus that follow, rightly or wrongly, compatibility rules within courses, and in many instances following compatibilities that are more or less classic and traditional: the chicken and hominy of Menu 1; the pork chops and applesauce of Menu 2; the curry of chicken and rice of Menu 10; the pork spareribs and red cabbage of Menu 17. Once or twice, as any inventive menu maker should, these menus intentionally depart from the traditional combinations, as in the baked bananas with the sole of Menu 3, or the asparagus tips with the braised sweetbreads of Menu 28: the first deviation is classic in the practice of a famous Paris fish restaurant; the second, a departure from *Ris de veau, Clamart,* I found in a now rare book by a famous French chef (*Clamart,* in the title of any dish, refers to the peas that accompany it, so named for the Paris suburb where traditionally the best peas are grown).

A really good cook, when he comes to menu making, will bear in mind some other traditional considerations which can be briefly summarized. In general, he will probably prefer what might be called linear rather than horizontal menus: a main dish that has only one compatible accompaniment, for example, like those cited, rather than several which (horizontally) clutter the table and his clients' stomachs. He will even prefer some dishes in solitary splendor, the coquilles St. Jacques of Menu 21, accompanied at most by bread or rolls on which its sauce can be sopped up. He will include potatoes with his main dish only when they are its best accompaniment, as, for example, with the sole Marguéry of Menu 25.

He will distinguish between different meals, and offer some hors d'oeuvre at lunch, some soup at dinner, as the preliminary course. But he will not hesitate to vary this tradition, as in Menu 28, where an hors d'oeuvre, marinated mushrooms, is proposed as a clarifying preliminary to braised sweetbreads and asparagus tips. He will tend to feel happier if fish figures somehow in an otherwise meaty meal, because his training, in sturdier days, leaves him with vestigial feelings that any proper meal should include both fish and meat; but he will be willing to relegate the fish to a soup, as, for example, in the cream of shrimp proposed as a preliminary to the pork spareribs of Menu 17. But he will not insist that every dinner must begin with a soup, as a Boston lady once did, in her shocked refusal to allow her scholarly husband to serve a stag dinner in her house without it, on a classic Roman menu, in which he supposed, on the basis of his research, no soup could be included.

Your really good cook will take it slightly amiss if having ordered one dish you say you want no salad, because he believes he has learned that a salad is essential to start flowing the liver juices that are required for the digestion of his fine main course. He will not be unhappy, however, if you succumb to none of the temptations he can offer as desserts, and even if you tell him that you prefer nothing beyond the salad save a fine coffee (and a brandy), though he would probably think more of your taste if you called for the finest fruit that was in season. As a cook justifiably proud of his products, he will be a bit happier if he can tempt you with some dessert, one which in his opinion contrasts a bit and still is compatible with what you have eaten—and with your weight. For both reasons, the desserts he may suggest may not be those you might have thought of: they will tend to be simpler (a mere stewed fruit), more seemingly ordinary (a *riz au lait*), more complicated, and more difficult than you might have thought he (or you) would wish to undertake (crêpes suzette). For these reasons, I have not included in the "Thirty Menus" of Part II, or in the desserts of Part III, "A la Carte" (see pp. 184 to 194) such desserts as ice cream and pie.

8. SERVING

The way any dish looks when it goes on the table is as much the cook's business as cooking or shopping. In a great restaurant, the chef, after having given his final decorative touches to a dish, may well from the service door watch to see how it is received at the table; and the maître d'hôtel, if he is proud of its appearance, as the chef may rightfully expect him to be, will "display" it to the guests before it is actually served them. It would, therefore, be false, amateur modesty, if the cook of his own meal did not allow himself similar satisfactions.

In serving, contrast perhaps overrules compatibility, at least in terms of color. This has been implicit in the make-up of the best classic cookbooks since color photography and fine color reproductions became possible, as in the case of *L'Art Culinaire Français* and its English version, which, incidentally, both have the same color plates. By comparison, the black-and-white illustrations of the older cookbooks of the same kind suggest little in this regard. They give the form, but not the essence.

Verbally, cookbooks have always lingered hopefully on the rich browns. All too seldom, in black and white, have they emphasized the other colors which are characteristic of good cookery when best displayed. To start the spectrum at the red end, you have beets (those of the boiled dinner of Menu 16), the carrots of the same meal; you have a wide range of really green vegetables, and when you lack them, for green, you always have just-sprinkled parsley, or green watercress as garnishing; blues, somehow, are poisonous in cookery, except in the artificially colored concoctions of the pastry cooks' violet petals; purples likewise are absent, save as the browns begin in them, as often do the richer wine sauces (none in this book); but the browns of cookery, like its golden yellows from frying, are almost spectra in themselves. The cook's palette, then, has gaps, but still permits pictures worthy of color photography and color reproductions in reds, oranges, yellows (as in the pure yellows of lemon garnishings), a broad range of greens, and browns.

Preferably your painting appears in a single frame, so that it can be appreciated as an integral work of art, embodying the two considerations of compatibility and contrast—as, for example, with the veal chops and stuffed tomatoes of Menu 15: the burned brown of the quickly cooked chops contrasting with the still bright red baked tomatoes stuffed with a cooked duxelles which has in the baking turned a darker brown than the chops, all bound together by the bright green of just-sprinkled chopped parsley, appear together on a single platter. In general, it is aesthetically preferable to serve a given course in one serving dish than to have a multiplicity of dishes—again hewing to the linear line of menu making, rather than to the horizontal clutter of many dishes.

Thus the chef in a fine restaurant, before watching from the service door, had watched the service in detail: if the waiter in ladling out the soup had allowed drops of it to spill on the edge of the soup plate, he had been reprimanded; the chef may well even have shifted an oyster or two on their platter of crushed ice, merely to augment a bit the composition of the picture; it was certainly he who saw to it that the asparagus tips were in a proper fan at the ends of the platter with the braised sweetbreads; most of all, it was he who, before any guest arrived, surveyed the setting of the buffet, hot or cold, of Menu 30.

There are, of course, other frames than a single platter—for example, the salad bowl: if you are offering a salad of lettuce and watercress, the composition of your picture is evidently more interesting if in laboring it you labor the lettuce first around the edges and the watercress into the center, into a symphony in greens.

Again, in the case of desserts, your apricots Condé of Menu 25 are enhanced both by their regular arrangement on their bed of *riz au lait* and by the pointillism of the candied fruitcake fruits that you scatter judiciously over them.

As in the case of building in flavor, however, it is quite as important to know when *not* as when *to* decorate. It is possible to decorate the clear brown of the mousse of chocolate of Menu 30 with dabs of sour or whipped cream. In Menu 30 they are not mentioned.

9. WINE, COFFEE . . . AND TEA

Wine, coffee, but, less, tea, are in the cook's picture. Yet all three are so related to good cookery in nonprofessional kitchens as to be almost an integral part of it.

Wine. This is to be no treatise; rather, I hope, only a few sensible remarks. I acknowledge enjoying the best wines and to having a certain taste in them. At the same time, I like wine generically, in meals, and in cookery. If the choice is between having a fine wine occasionally, or ordinary wine constantly, I opt for the latter. In simple, economic terms, this option means for most of us, if you want wine at every proper meal, and if you want to use it freely in cookery, American wines, and, further, the American wines that come in gallon jugs.

There are worse fates. Actually, if one looks about, he can almost always now find both red and white American wines in gallon jugs that are as good if not better than the celebrated European *vins ordinaires*. Their makers may be careless, and if two gallons of a wine you have come to think yours turn out to be bad, look for another. To give such wines a fair chance, accumulate four quart bottles, or five fifths, preferably, for convenience, with screw tops; wash them well and as you open a gallon of wine, bottle it off in them: wine spoils more rapidly in proportion to the amount of air (with its concomitant content of wild yeasts) to which it is exposed; if you pour off what you use from the original gallon jug, the proportion of air (and wild yeasts) increases; if you keep it in separate bottles, the proportion is minimized.

Our guests, a certain number of whom are true amateurs of wine, gladly drink these ordinary American wines at our table. Furthermore, their low cost allows us to serve them at the table and to use them in cookery ad lib. Finally, it has always seemed that a real ability to appreciate fine wines depends, fundamentally, on drinking more ordinary wines customarily, in order that you may have a well-established base for appreciating exceptional qualities.

In the menus that follow, therefore, wine is simply wine, red wine, white wine, occasionally a light red wine, or a red wine of the Burgundy type. If you know good wines, you can yourself think of one which would suit a given meal; if not, you can consult a knowing friend, or a really reliable wineseller. If you want a really fine wine, steel yourself to pay for it, and at the best vintner's. There are few real bargains in fine wines.

These same remarks apply as well to the richer and stronger wines, sherry, port, madeira, and marsala. Recently there have appeared some California sherries at reasonable prices usually not in gallon but half-gallon jugs, which are quite reputable for preprandial drinking and for use in cookery. I have yet to find equally reputable American ports, but they may exist. If you buy a wine of this type especially for cooking, as I do, I recommend for better flavor the sweeter, fuller, cream sherries, or, best of all, the California marsalas modeled on the Italian, sherry-like wine of that name.

Coffee. This may be still a minority report, but time appears to be on its side. One of our national clichés is that European coffee is awful. I have been in a minority in happening to prefer it to ours. In general, European coffee is made strong from high-roasted coffee, i.e., coffee that is roasted not until it is merely brown, but, rather, black and oily. When the first version of this book was written, this kind of coffee could be readily bought, ground to be sure, in only one brand with an Italian name. Now there are a number which advertise themselves as a "demitasse coffee." Thus the taste for high-roasted coffee seems to be taking hold. There were times when a certain number of our guests left theirs only partly drunk. More recently the rule has been for them to mention how much they like it, and to ask how it can be procured and made.

The answer is buy black oily coffee in the bean, as you can at any shop that specializes in coffee or in better Italian groceries; grind it immediately before making (we have a small and most efficient French electric coffee grinder); make your coffee in a porcelain pot with a porcelain filter top, known as a biggin; and use plenty of coffee. Admittedly, this is a bothersome procedure, but in my view well worth the bother. To follow it, you have to boil water for the coffee in one pan, and to keep it hot have the porcelain pot sitting in its own pan of hot water. But the inert porcelain does not affect the coffee's flavor; admitting that coffee made at the last minute tastes a little better, I make it in such a pot while I am preparing a meal, well ahead of its actual serving, and with little deterioration in flavor; finally what is left after dinner serves perfectly well for breakfast the morning after, particularly when drunk with half a cup of hot milk instead of cream, as Europeans in any case prefer their breakfast coffee.

For years I was twitted by more conformist friends for insisting on after-dinner or after-luncheon coffee in small cups, the "wicked demitasses" of the limerick. There is usually a reason for such preferences, and at last I found it: good coffee is truly, to give the hackneyed saw its last squeal, black as Sin, strong as the Devil, and hot as Hell. Blackness comes from high roasting; strength comes from using plenty; and heat comes from the demitasse, which, with its smaller radiating surface, seems to have the characteristic of keeping its modicum of coffee hot as Hell.

Contrariwise, breakfast coffee with its hot milk is, as the French regard it, more a nourishing drink, almost like a breakfast soup. It is better drunk in a large cup, warm, rather than hot; at home, the French drink it in bowls.

Having been dogmatic on this subject, let me be more realistic. Some years ago I was told of some so-called research which seemed to indicate that tastes in coffee are hereditary: some genes take to a given coffee; some don't. Thus a coffee flavor that may be delicious to some is near nauseating to others. Whatever coffee suits your taste, hereditary or otherwise, will, however, benefit from being made strong and by some process that doesn't filter out the finer particles that give it body.

The retention of these particles is of course the secret of the fine flavor and quality of so-called Turkish coffee, made by boiling up three times in a long-handled cuplike pot coffee that has been powdered, letting it settle a bit, and pouring it off in a cup where still more of the powder settles in its bottom. It is likewise the secret of the finest coffee I have ever drunk, Arab coffee. Its making, while almost a ritual for anthropologists, sums up what seem the principles of fine coffee making. Green coffee beans are roasted in a kind of spoon over a Bedouin fire. They are then pounded to powder in a small mortar, with the rhythmic tinkle of the metal pestle an integral part of the process. To the powdered coffee in a necessarily metal pot is added not water but the coffee that remains from the last making, with just enough more water to yield the required amount. It is then boiled up three times, and served a hot tablespoonful at a time in tiny handleless cups. You are, understandably, supposed to take no more than three. Black, strong, and hot, its pungency sets a standard anyone who has drunk it will always try to achieve for himself.

Tea. While tea has no legitimate place in good cookery at the luncheon or dinner table, it has a certain relation to both meals, most evident when you have attended an official luncheon in France with wines and brandy afterward, and are destined for a similar meal at dinner: on such a day, tea toward four-thirty or five is essential to clear the mind and stomach. The British are likewise sagacious in using it as an eye opener in the morning.

Too few Americans know how good tea can be, and for what may be a valid reason. Tea at its best, with few exceptions, is one type of tea. Rightly or wrongly it is said that American tea packagers fear creating a taste for any given tea in the United States: the American market for it is so huge that if a taste developed for any given tea, there would be hardly enough of it to meet the demand. Whatever the reason, teas generally available in the United States are blends.

It is less and less difficult, however, to find teas of given types, if you take the trouble to look for them. I usually have two or three in the house, one a smoky Lapsang Suchong, which seems particularly good in the afternoon; sometimes a Formosa Oolong, good then and in the morning; occasionally an Indian Darjeeling, rich and comforting either in the morning or the afternoon; and a morning tea that may well be a blend, called Kee Mun or English Breakfast. Finally there is one outright blend that sets a standard of its own, Earl Grey's Mixture, always expensive in the United States, but well worth what you pay.

Give whatever tea you use a chance to be at its best: preheat the pot with boiling water; when the water with which you will make the tea begins to boil, pour off the water in the pot, put in it a teaspoonful of tea for each cup you want, traditionally with one more "for the pot," pour the freshly boiling water over it, and let it "draw" for at least three minutes, better five. Stir before pouring.

10. THE KITCHEN

The preceding pages have dealt primarily with the first two of the three principles of good cookery, *having the best ingredients*, and *cooking them to bring out their best*. Most of what this book will have to say of the third principle, *minimizing, or, better, avoiding, the difficulties* in so cooking them appears in the detailed directions of Parts II and III. But a means toward that end is a well-organized kitchen with a certain minimum of equipment.

All the cooking implied in Parts II and III has been carried on for more than ten years in a minimum New York apartment kitchen with no more equipment than presently will be listed. This kitchen at its broadest point is four feet six inches wide and eight feet in length from the refrigerator door at its inner end to the window at its outer end. Its walking surface is just three by eight feet. It has the great advantage of being a one-way kitchen: with the refrigerator door at the left, one need not turn to work at the ample kitchen shelf, the sink, or the stove by the window. The southern exposure of the window facilitates the growth of herbs in a windowbox on its sill when the growing season is right for them: thyme, marjoram, basil, chives, and, betimes, tarragon, by far the hardest to catch on, indoors. Dill and parsley can readily be grown in such a box, but they take so much space in it that it is preferable to buy them. The refrigerator is one that is now fairly standard, with a small freezing unit and a vegetable drawer. The stove, whose top is twenty inches square, has four gas burners, so closely placed that with medium-sized saucepans they can hardly all be used at the same time. It has a small but adequate oven, with a broiler above the stove's top, where I prefer it, approximately at eye level, and where it accumulates the heat from the top burners and ovens, so that, when unlit, it is useful for warming plates and serving dishes. Whatever the kitchen designers say, I am convinced that such a kitchen includes the essentials of kitchen efficiency: it is "one-way," and it has working space on its ample shelf.

On the left hand, inner side of my shelf is an electric Mixmaster, with meat-grinder and egg-beating attachments; a bottle each of olive oil, vinegar, red and white wine for cooking (usually unfinished bottles from the table), and a bottle of marsala. Along the back of the shelf are garlic, salt, a pepper grinder, and measuring cups. In the middle of the shelf at the back is one of those small alarm-clock contraptions called a Minute Minder which, when set at any point between one and sixty minutes, rings a bell when the period has run out, essential if you will submit to the timing indicated in Parts II and III.

In such a kitchen you need, in this book, only a minimum of equipment. The following list is minimum but entirely adequate for anything this book requires.

A chef's knife: mine has an 8½-inch blade that is straight on its cutting edge almost to its tip; the straight edge is important particularly for chopping, for example herbs on a cutting board, best done with such a knife tapped quickly from a relaxed wrist; or other vegetables, holding the top of the blade in your two hands; it is equally good for slicing meats or vegetables; in fact, it is the only knife I ordinarily use.

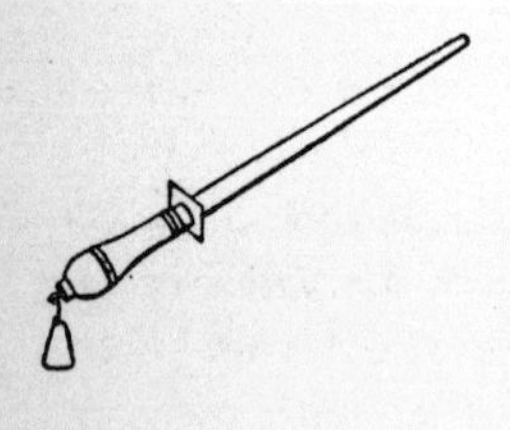

A steel: for keeping this and other knives sharp; ask your butcher to show you how he uses his for this purpose; if you can learn the trick, you will rarely need to have your knives otherwise sharpened.

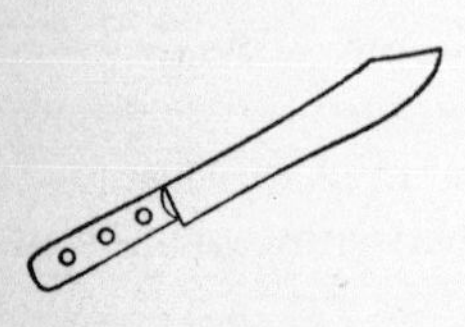

A sturdy knife: some heavy knife, it does not matter much what, that you can use for operations that require more force than sharpness, and which hence conserves the sharpness of your other knives, e.g., for opening lobsters.

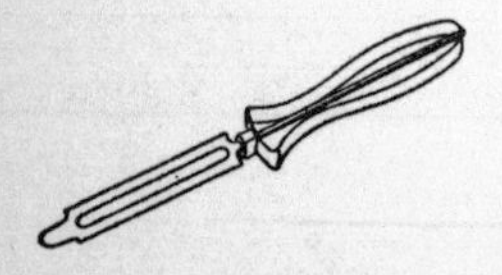

A peeling knife: the preferred kind is one that peels thinly through a sharpened slit in the middle of its blade.

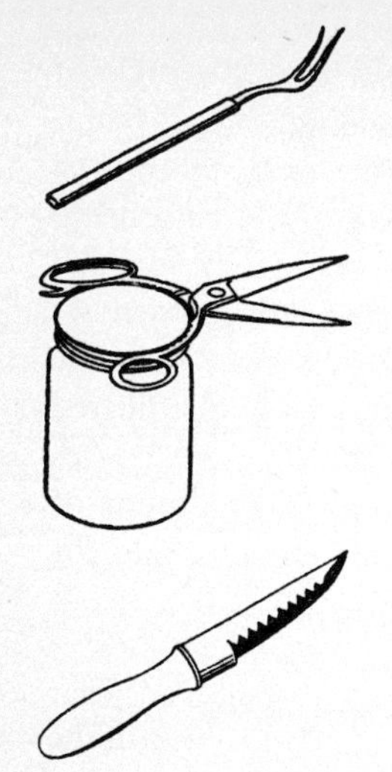

A two-tined fork: for dealing with meats in the broiler, "folding in" beaten egg whites, and a variety of other uses. And keep its tines sharp: so doing will save you time in that, if sharp, they won't stick in meats.

Kitchen scissors: particularly useful are the stout pointed scissors with corrugations on the inner handle stems that quickly open recalcitrant screw bottle and jar tops.

An apple corer: for a variety of uses larger than its name implies.

Wooden spoons: at least three; small, medium, and large; once you have become accustomed to them you will use no others; they never get hot, are soft on pans, and wash easily.

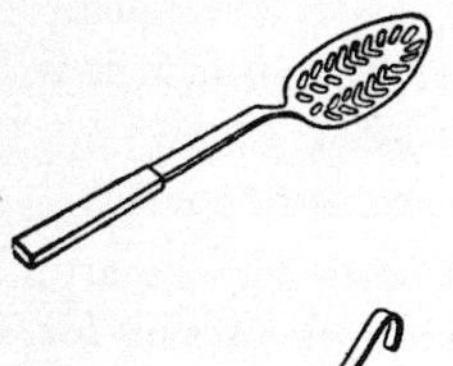

A metal perforated spoon: for lifting things out of hot liquids, and for beating.

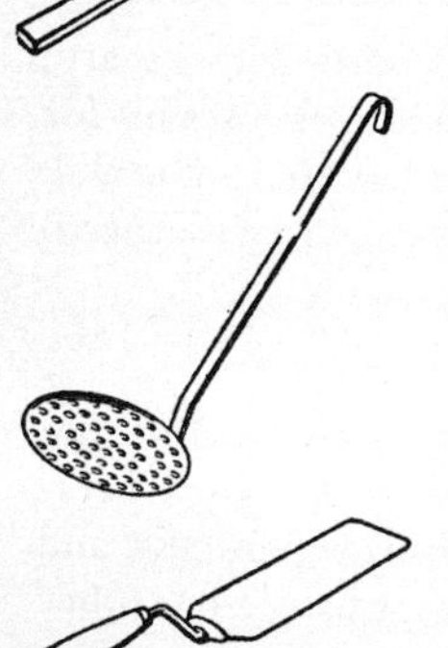

A skimmer: particularly for skimming sauces and soups, but quite as essential for a variety of other uses, as, for example, lifting a roast bird, or even a ham, from its baking pan.

A broad spatula (or pancake turner): preferably the longer, narrower type.

A trussing needle: for trussing poultry; best is a 6-inch sailmaker's needle which you can find in better hardware shops.

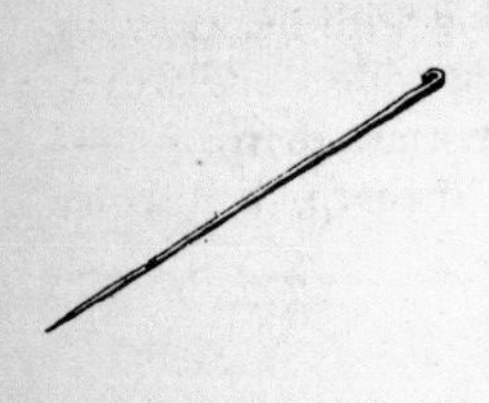

Spits: particularly in this book for Menus 7 and 8, but otherwise useful, as in Menu 2; the best spits are square, to minimize the rotation of whatever you put on them; if you can't readily buy them, you can make them, or get them made, from heavy galvanized iron wire, or more prettily from heavy copper wire.

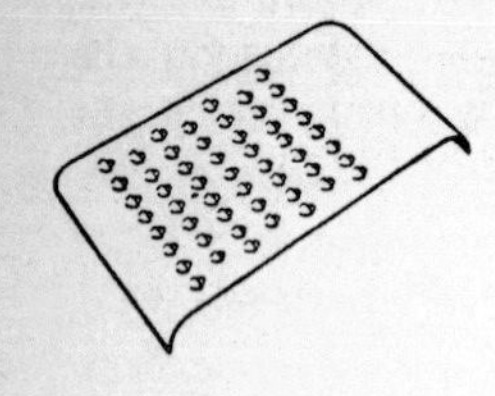

Graters: preferably the ones that lie flat, one fine, one medium.

A wire sieve: medium-sized, but fine meshed.

A colander: of aluminum, or white enamel for easier washing.

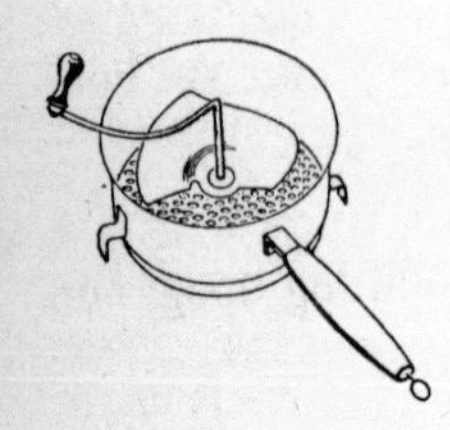

A Foley Food Mill: an indispensable implement, generally procurable under this name at hardware shops and department stores: a kind of saucepan with a corrugated sieve for its bottom over which a handle turns a blade to force through purées. I prefer it to electric "blenders" which seem to me to "blend" into a paste rather than to "purée."

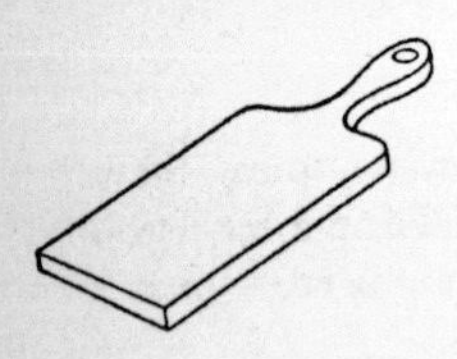

A chopping board: preferably oblong with a handle, for chopping herbs, etc., with your chef's knife and a variety of other uses, e.g., serving cheese that is to be sliced on the table.

An egg beater: preferably an electric beater, but it's also handy to have a hand beater for quick uses.

A meat grinder: your Mixmaster may include the attachment; if not, a hand grinder serves quite as well.

Beating bowls: at least two, one small enough to fit within the larger, if only to be able to put ice in the larger one when you make mayonnaise.

Measuring spoons: quarter-, half-, teaspoon, and tablespoon.

Measuring cups: two are handy.

Oven thermometer: unless your stove has one built in.

Timer: of the Minute-Minder variety referred to above, again, unless your stove has one built in.

Paper towels: for liberal use in all kinds of drying.

Wax paper: principally for convenience when you work with flour or bread crumbs.

Aluminum foil: principally for preserving foods in the refrigerator.

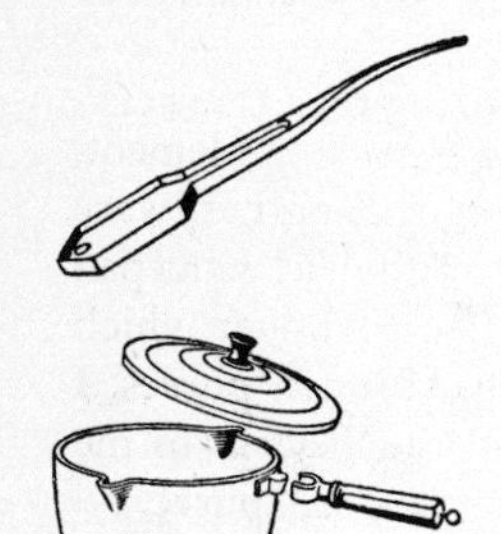

A shrimp deveiner: invaluable if you deal with fresh shrimps as much as this book suggests: inserted along their backs, it neatly removes both the shell and the intestinal strip at the same time.

Saucepans: at least one small, two medium, one large sized. I have come to prefer the heavy cast aluminum pans with covers and removable handles that make them equally usable on the top of the stove and in the oven.

Frying pans: at least one, preferably two, one smaller, the other larger, likewise of cast aluminum, with covers and removable handles, for the same reasons.

Double boilers: two, one smaller for ordinary uses, one of two-quart capacity for cream soups and other uses.

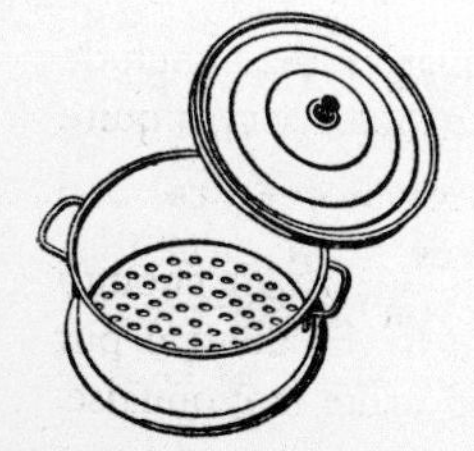

A steamer: a perforated kettle in which vegetables can be steamed over water in a saucepan.

A soup kettle: a straight-sided kettle of aluminum or enamelware, from ten to twelve inches in diameter.

Oven pans: oblong: two, one smaller, one larger, of pyrex glass that can be used as serving dishes.

Cocottes: the round, brown-glazed porcelain dishes, with covers, in which oven-cooked dishes are attractively served at the table.

Pie plates: round, one smaller, one larger, preferably of pyrex.

A roasting pan: preferably with a cover and a rack on which roasts can conveniently be lifted out; mine is of light aluminum. While you are getting one, it's well to buy one as large as your oven will accommodate.

Custard cups: preferably of pyrex, for occasional uses, e.g., for baked eggs.

Scallop shells: the natural article, now available in most kitchen and department stores.

Molds: primarily in this book for aspics (see p. 177). The individual molds are easier to use, but you may wish to experiment with one larger one, as, for example, with a mousse of ham (see p. 180).

Ball (or Mason) jars: for preserving sauces, etc., in the refrigerator. Three of the pint size and three of the quart size should serve. They should be heat resistant to take sauces at boiling temperature, and should have sturdy screw tops for tight sealing.

Other refrigerator containers: as you will. Someday someone will standardize them, probably in square dishes, with covers, so that they will take a minimum of refrigerator space, and will be usable for serving dishes, as, for example, for *hors d'oeuvres variés* when you happily involve yourself in a summer "run" of them, as is suggested below (p. 142).

A "butter" brush: a small brush, like a paint-brush, preferably now with artificial fibers so that it can be washed quite clean, for a variety of uses other than buttering.

A vegetable brush: any cheap scrub brush that will, e.g., get the clinging dirt out of asparagus tips.

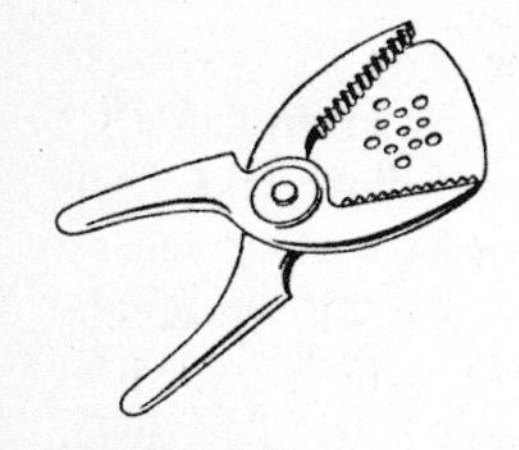

A lemon squeezer: as you prefer; one of the barman's type, with its built-in strainer, is for me the handiest.

A toaster: you need not have one, but most do: you can, if you lack one, equally well toast bread under the broiler.

At first reading this may well seem to you a formidable list for *minimum* kitchen equipment. Yet, if you now have a kitchen, a rapid check of the equipment you have against this list will show you that you have accumulated most of it, but, I suspect, that you have not two, or three, or four items that would really make your work in the kitchen much easier. If you already have a kitchen and its equipment, go on for a while with both as they are. Gradually modify what you have in the light of these remarks, and see how progressively your kitchen becomes more efficient. If you are about to acquire a kitchen and its equipment, these remarks may be helpful in telling you what you will want, initially, and lastingly.

Finally, there are three other implements which are invaluable in any kitchen: your two hands and your nose. Most cooks do far too little with their bare hands. It took me some time, for example, to recognize that I could best mold *pâté de foie gras* for aspics (see Menu 19) with my fingers, washed before and afterward under the nearby faucet in the sink. As you go on in good cookery, see how much more you can use your hands and fingers than you are inclined to. Your nose, likewise, can become a most sensitive indicator. It usually tells you, before any thermometer can, that something in the oven is going too fast, i.e., is near to burning. And in many instances the smell of things is as good if not a better indicator of flavor than the tongue. Learn to depend on it.

Any really good cook, particularly a man, should be determined to refute the persistent rumor that his efforts in the kitchen result in a mess of what are, in boardinghouse parlance, known as "stinkers," i.e., thoroughly dirty cooking dishes. Actually, as you have seen, really good cookery results in virtually clean frying pans, because it utilizes all the "glaze." But it is really easier on the cook (his working space is kept clear) to wash cooking dishes as he goes along, and to put them away, or, better, to use them again, as you often can after a quick rinsing. As you will see, the menus that follow take pride in calling for a minimum number of cooking utensils.

Standing at your kitchen shelf, in a small "one-way" kitchen, you will develop quick and efficient methods of your own for performing the standard cooking procedures. I'll cite merely a few suggestive examples.

Chopping parsley or other herbs. There are, of course, all kinds of chopping gadgets; but none of them is, in the long run, so quick or effective as a chopping board and your straight-edged chef's knife. Take the designated number of stalks of parsley and, holding the leafy ends together with the fingers of your left hand, cut them off the resulting bunch with the chef's knife in your right hand. Cut once this way, more or less finely, they can be quickly reduced to finely chopped parsley by the same knife, tapped rapidly on them from a relaxed wrist—if you have just sharpened it with the steel.

Chopping onions, carrots, etc. Unless you want small, reasonably regular pieces for looks as in sauce vinaigrette (see p. 174), such "chopping" is most quickly and effectively accomplished by grating: for sauces, soups, etc., for which onions and carrots are most frequently required, put your fine or medium grater over the saucepan in which you are to cook them, and grate them directly into it. If the pan in question isn't ready for them, why not grate them directly on to the kitchen shelf? Watch good cooks at work in some restaurant that allows you to see them at work: they will spend an appreciable part of the time during which you watch them keeping clean whatever working surface they use. Why not follow their example?

Reusing utensils: When cooking, why not see, first, how few utensils you can use? Then see how many, perhaps with rinsing, you can use again. For example, in the seemingly complicated procedure of making *crêpes suzette* of Menu 19 (see p. 192), you can perfectly well fry your *crêpes* and serve them in the same frying pan.

These are, intentionally, only a few of the tricks that any really good cook develops for himself—intentionally, because you should develop them for yourself, if, as one hopes, you are to be a really good cook.

I got started on this track in a way that it may be helpful to repeat. In earlier days, when help (to use the New England term) was easier to get and relatively inexpensive, for several vacations in Maine we enjoyed the services of a Pullman porter, who had what he regarded as his vacation cooking for us there. Like many aging Pullman porters, his "feet were bad," and he used to spend much of his free time sitting on our little pier soaking them in the soft water of the lake. He saved them, too, as he had learned to in the cramped quarters of a Pullman galley, by standing in our small kitchen, as much as he could, in one spot. I can see him still, squeezing oranges for our breakfast orange juice (this was before the days of prepared juice), not moving his feet, but tossing the dejuiced skins unerringly into an open garbage pail eight feet away; or turning to jiggle the eggs frying on the top of the stove (he always cooked them too fast), or even pulling open the oven door to see how the muffins were doing, still without moving his feet. You will find that you can save yourself enormously by such dodges, particularly in today's small kitchens. In fact, when you have the hang of cooking in one, you wouldn't take the gift of anything larger.

11. AND WITH A CLEAR CONSCIENCE...

One constant reaction to this book in its earlier version indicates the need of the following remarks.

This constant reaction focused on butter, with two variants. "How can you eat all that butter and not get fat?" "You use so much butter that your arteries must be hardening fast from all its cholesterol."

Perhaps they are, but the author's blood pressure is supposedly normal for his age. Admittedly he is a ripe fifty-five and has to watch his weight. Six feet two and a half inches tall, he has on this diet touched 195. Also, he has reduced without too much trouble to 180. His comfortable and proper weight seems to be 190, as any medical man would readily agree. He can easily maintain a weight of 190 on the diet this book projects. How?

First, by eating less. If food is good, really flavorful, eating less of it is easier: a little by its quality compensates for much more. Your author learned this the one time he touched 195. Confronted with the problem, one of his sagacious medical friends asked, "How many eggs do you eat for breakfast?" "Two." "Try one." It worked, even with one ostensibly rich scrambled egg. If you have been accustomed to two of anything, try one, and dwell on its enjoyment: generally eat half of what you ate before the swelling years came on you.

Second, by minimizing your consumption of bread. You will remark that this book mentions bread only in a meal or two where it undeniably makes the best accompaniment for the dish in question, as, for example, in Menu 18, when you need it for the Swiss fondue. And even when it is essential, bread need not be accompanied by butter. Actually, it is at its best with other things, sauces, for example. And one is no longer looked down on in the United States for using a piece of bread to sop up the remnants of some fine sauce.

As for cholesterol, you can hardly avoid it in any diet unless you go in for one that is really meager, both in the technical sense of a Lenten diet and in terms of flavor. And it will be so meager in the latter sense of flavor that it will be hard indeed for you to eat less. Virtually all the fine flavors of food are fat-borne. An otherwise fine-appearing piece of steak without striated fat through the lean will be tasteless for this reason, as will a soup that lacks adequate fat in its preparation. And the fat that carries and contributes flavor best is butter, the best butter.

If you limit your use of butter to cooking where it does the most good, and abjure it on the table, particularly with bread, you will find that in cooking a week through the meals this book suggests your total consumption of butter will not exceed what is allowed by the most extreme cholesterol faddist.

So enjoy good eating, in satisfying smaller quantities, with a clear conscience.

PART II

THIRTY MENUS

REQUIRED READING

Part I of this book, "Good Cookery," is intended only to be read. Parts II and III, "Thirty Menus" and "A la Carte," respectively, are intended both to be read and to be used.

They are to be read just as one reads a restaurant bill of fare, to choose what you want to eat. Thus, in "Thirty Menus" you will find thirty complete meals (dinners, luncheons, suppers, and one buffet) centering in some dish with its appropriate accompaniments, just as many restaurants feature some "special for the day." In "A la Carte," as on restaurant bills of fare, you will find the preliminaries and sequels to these dishes, and other special dishes (*spécialités de la maison*) with which you can construct meals that whet the appetite of the moment.

Parts II and III are also to be used to prepare for yourself and your guests the meals you choose. They provide precise directions for the preparation of each dish included, precise as to what to use, how much to use, how to use it, and when. Parts II and III will mean more to you both in reading and in use if you have read Part I. But to use Parts II and III intelligently, it is *absolutely requisite* first to read these brief introductory pages.

What to use. What you will need to buy for each of the thirty menus is clearly indicated in their shopping lists. But these lists assume that you have in the house the following minimum supplies:

Staples **(things that keep indefinitely)**

Flour	1 pound.
Arrowroot flour	1 pound: this is an essential of good cookery, which can be found in better grocers, in herb shops, or in really professional pharmacies, since it is sometimes called for in pharmacopoeia; and while you're getting it, you might just as well get a pound, or at least a half pound.
Sugar (granulated)	1 pound.

Staples **(things that keep indefinitely) (*Cont.*)**

Sugar (powdered)	1 pound.
Sugar (brown)	1 pound.
Rice	1 pound.
Raisins	1 pound of the seedless variety.
Bread crumbs	1 can.
Consommé (beef)	4 ten-ounce cans.
Consommé (chicken)	2 ten-ounce cans.
Tomato paste	1 six-ounce tin, and those made by Italian makers (in Italy or America) are to be preferred.
Oil	1 quart, preferably olive oil which now is reasonable in price.
Vinegar	3 bottles: red wine vinegar; white wine vinegar flavored with tarragon, and from the stalk of tarragon that now usually comes in it, a source of tarragon leaves; an ordinary cider vinegar for less important uses, e.g., in sauces.
Salt	1 pound: I have come to prefer Kosher salt; it is pure salt and therefore standard; its relatively big grains don't stick even in humid weather and look pretty in uses where they show.
Pepper	a pepper grinder filled with white or black whole pepper, with a jar of whole peppers in reserve.
Cayenne pepper	1 can of the ordinary.
Paprika	1 can of the ordinary, or better of some of the fine Hungarian varieties that can be found in specialized grocery or herb shops.
Mustard	1 small can of dry mustard of any good variety. Mustard rapidly loses its full flavor when moistened. It is therefore preferable to "prepare" your own as you want it. Flavored vinegars are particularly good as moisteners, and a few drops to a tablespoonful of dry mustard suffices. The addition of sugar heightens the flavor and makes the mixture blander.

Thyme	1 can or jar, preferably not powdered but in broken leaves.
Marjoram	1 can or jar, again in broken leaves.
Bay leaves	1 small can or jar.
Cloves	1 small can or jar of whole cloves.
Nutmeg	1 nutmeg grater (which can readily be found in department and kitchen stores) and one jar of whole nutmegs.
Vanilla beans	2: to be kept moist, they should be kept in a tube or bottle; to be most effective in use the prescribed length should be slit with a knife, and the tiny seeds scraped into the dish which calls for its flavor.
Vegetable fat	1 pound.
Gelatin	in the unflavored, crystalline form, which usually comes in one-ounce envelopes.

Perishables

Milk	1 quart.
Cream	1 half-pint: unless for coffee, I prefer the homogenized sour cream, smooth and sweet in taste, which keeps much longer.
Eggs	1 dozen.
Butter	1 pound.
Carrots	1 bunch.
Onions	2 pounds.
Shallots	1 small basket: their flavor, more delicate than onions, makes them distinctly preferable for purposes for which chopped onions can be used; they are now more frequently available in better vegetable shops than most suppose.
Garlic	1 whole root, preferably one with big cloves.
Parsley	1 bunch: I used to think that the broad-leafed Italian variety gave more flavor, but the curly variety is more easily chopped.
Lemons	2.

Perishables (Cont.)

Mayonnaise	1 small jar (for less important uses: otherwise you will make your own).

Wines for cooking

Sherry type	any inexpensive American variety will serve, though the finer the sherry, the more flavor it imparts. Once given a bottle of a very choice but very sweet sherry which I do not like, I surreptitiously used it for flavoring aspics and soups with results that everyone remarked. For cookery, the sweeter, richer sherries are distinctly preferable. I have come to depend on California Marsala, modeled on the Italian counterpart to sherry.
Red wine	the remains of a bottle that has not been entirely consumed on the table; this is not an unworthy fate for the remains of even fine table wines.
White wine	ditto.

Spirits

In this book brandy, whisky, and some liqueur are occasionally called for. Most won't begrudge the equivalent of a drink of whisky in cooking now and then. But I admit to drawing back from the similar use of a fine brandy or a fine liqueur. For brandy, the best solution is to buy a small bottle of some relatively inexpensive California brandy which for all but the most sensitive palates is quite as good as the better varieties, particularly when its principal function is flaming. One can also fabricate an inexpensive all-purpose liqueur for cooking by buying a bottle of the least expensive vodka and putting into it the peel of one or more oranges, or even lemon peel. It probably does not impart quite so fine a flavor to *crêpes suzette*, for example, as the required mixture of brandy, Grand Marnier and curaçao, but one's pocketbook is the better for its use. I now substitute for cherry brandy (kirsch) the extra juice from the cherries in "brandy"—in vodka (see p. 187); its deep red coloration makes it aesthetically a little less attractive on fruits and in Swiss fondue than its pure white Swiss counterpart. But otherwise it serves.

How much to use. Thinking they know how much to use gives some cooks the impression of being "creative" in the kitchen. But really experienced cooks see through this illusion: most of them make their dry measurements by weight, the only really accurate method, in French cookery, in grams. But since sensitive kitchen scales are hard to come by in the United States, I have transposed dry measurements into the most exact American measurements: the standard American cup and spoonfuls. Liquid measurement by cups and quarts is fortunately as accurate as in the French liters and deciliters. I have ventured one innovation which I hope will prove advantageous for others as it has for me: the measurement of solid butter in cubic inches. Unless butter is melted, its measurement by cup or spoon is downright inconvenient. On the other hand, almost every American has clearly in mind the standard quarter-pound bar, an inch square and five inches long: an inch off this bar yields one cubic inch. With this standard in mind, anyone can readily learn to measure butter, whether from a bar or from a block of the tub butter that I prefer. Certainly this measurement of butter is better than the hackneyed but precarious term, "butter the size of a walnut."

How to use it. On this score the aim throughout is real precision. Thus the directions are as "operational" as possible, telling you, for example, how this or that should look at a given point in its cooking, or warning you how things might go wrong, and advising you what you can do to avoid their going wrong.

When to use it. As remarked in the Introduction, good cookery usually falls into two distinct phases: the preparation of the ingredients and the actual cooking. The directions for the "Thirty Menus" are accordingly given under these two headings. In some instances preparations can be undertaken well in advance; for a dinner, for example, in the morning, or even the evening of the previous day. Some of them, if you prefer, can be deferred till during the actual cooking. In general, however, it is better to complete them before the cooking begins, if only that you may give it your undivided attention, and, undistracted, find in it the enjoyment it can afford. The actual cooking, on the other hand, more often than not depends on timing for its excellence. When heat and quantities are standard, most dishes are at their best when cooked just so long. The timings of these menus are the outcome of long experimentation in that regard. Furthermore, if a dish is to be at its best when it is eaten, its cooking must begin just so long before zero-hour, mealtime. Finally, when you have learned to depend on timing, you will find the pressures of cooking much diminished, and thus again come to enjoy it more. The timing of these menus is given in minutes (occasionally in hours) before the scheduled mealtime, in bold-face type at the right: they have been kept to a minimum; hence each noted is essential for full success.

This timing, however, assumes (1) that you will allow time for the preparation of any preliminary (*hors d'oeuvre* or soup), of any dessert, and the post-prandial coffee; (2) that you have cooked the dish in question at least once before (if you have not, allow a little longer, if only to provide the extra time you will need to study the directions); and (3) that you are cooking for the specified number of people: if you are cooking for more, allow a little longer, because actually cooking in larger quantities takes a little longer.

The "Thirty Menus" could have been arranged in the traditional order of the bill of fare, fish dishes first, etc. Instead, they are arranged in the interest of good reading. Menus 1 through 6 illustrate the variety of good cookery this book offers. Menus 7 through 10 continue this illustrative process with respect to four relatively exotic meals. Menus 11 through 17 attempt to tell you how meals you well know can be better cooked and so better eating. Menus 18 on move into the classic dishes of *haute cuisine* more or less in order of increasing complexity. But none of them is really difficult, as you will see when you try them. Indeed, some you might think the most difficult turn out to be the easiest.

In choosing a menu for a given occasion you will do well to take into account, along with its gustatory appeal, how practical it is for that occasion. For example, practical for a dinner on an occasion when you want to be free for undisturbed preprandial conversation or cocktails, or when you are asking some of your guests at a cocktail party to stay on for dinner would be Menu 16, the New England boiled dinner, which requires hardly any attention after early preparations until the moment it is served. Similarly, if you are coming in with a guest, and want a luncheon or a supper that can be on the table fifteen minutes later, Menu 18 provides it.

Finally, Parts II and III of this book assume that you have a certain minimum of equipment in your kitchen. What you are assumed to have is described in detail in Part I, pp. 37 to 45. As you go back to these pages to check what you have and lack, if you have not read Part I, browse in it a bit: it will make Parts II and III richer as you read and use them.

THE THIRTY MENUS

1.

CREAM OF CELERY
FRIED CHICKEN BERCY
HOMINY
FRUIT

2.

TOMATO BOUILLON
PORK CHOPS
APPLESAUCE
CHEESE

3.

OYSTERS
SOLE BANARO
BAKED BANANAS
OMELETTE FLAMBÉE

4.

SMOKED SALMON
VEAL IN CREAM
SPINACH
PINEAPPLE IN KIRSCH

5.

SCALLOPS MEUNIÈRE
FRENCH PEAS
STEWED PEARS

6.

HORS D'OEUVRES VARIÉS
MUSHROOMS MATINALE
CHEESE, FRUIT, AND NUTS

7.

TURKISH SWORDFISH
COOKED CUCUMBERS
SALAD
COLD CUTS
STEWED KUMQUATS

8.

BORSCHT
SHISH KEBAB
PILAF
APRICOTS AND ALMONDS

9.

ANTIPASTO
SPAGHETTI
RICOTTA

10.

HERRING IN WINE
CURRY OF CHICKEN
INDIAN RICE
MANGOES

11.

CREAM OF MUSHROOMS
LAMB CHOPS
PURÉE OF PEAS
BAKED APPLES BONNE FEMME

12.

ANCHOVIES ON TOAST
STEAK
BAKED POTATOES
CHEESE

13.

CREAM OF OYSTERS
ROAST CHICKEN
TURNIPS
CHERRIES (JUBILEE OR BRANDIED)

14.

POTAGE PARMENTIER
BAKED HAM
BRAISED ENDIVES
FRESH ORANGES IN CURAÇAO

15.

CREAM OF CORN
VEAL CHOPS
STUFFED TOMATOES
STEWED FRUIT

16.

NEW ENGLAND BOILED DINNER
INDIAN PUDDING

17.

CREAM OF SHRIMP
PORK SPARERIBS
RED CABBAGE
BERRIES

18.

OXTAIL SOUP
FONDUE

19.

PÂTÉ DE FOIE GRAS
ASPARAGUS HOLLANDAISE
CRÊPES SUZETTE

20.

STUFFED PANCAKES
ARTICHOKES VINAIGRETTE
RØD GRØD

21.

COQUILLES ST. JACQUES
AVOCADO SALAD
RIZ AU LAIT

22.

LOBSTER OR SHRIMP NEWBURG
ARTICHOKES
GINGER

23.

LOBSTER OR SHRIMP AMÉRICAINE
PILAF
BABAS AU RHUM

24.

DEVILED CRAB
SALADE BELLE HORTENSE
PÂTÉ DE FOIE GRAS IN ASPIC
FLAMED PEARS

25.

FILET OF SOLE MARGUÉRY
STEAMED POTATOES
APRICOTS CONDÉ

26.

CREAM OF PEAS
VEAL CHASSEUR
STRING BEANS
DATES FIGS NUTS

27.

FOIS GRAS
ROAST DUCK BIGARADE
WILD RICE
TURINOIS

28.

MARINATED MUSHROOMS
BRAISED SWEETBREADS
ASPARAGUS TIPS
STRAWBERRIES AND PINEAPPLE

29.

POTAGE OF WATER CRESS
BRAISED SHORT RIBS OF BEEF
CARROTS ONIONS
IMPERIAL PEARS

30.

GREEN TURTLE SOUP
BRAISED HAM
CELERY MORNAY
MOUSSE OF CHOCOLATE

Menu 1

Fried Chicken Bercy   Hominy

Dinner for two

AN EASY, quick meal, with chicken in a way new to most Americans.

Shopping list

1 small broiler, the smallest you can buy, split as if for broiling, with the backbone removed; ask the butcher to cut it into four pieces, breasts and wings, legs and thighs together.

1 can of hominy (white corn kernels, puffed by leaching); if you cannot find it, a can of whole-kernel corn will do.

½ lb. of mushrooms.

Salad, as you will.

Preparations

Chop enough parsley to yield two tablespoonfuls.

Peel and chop 3 shallots, or, if you haven't them, enough onions to yield 3 tablespoonfuls.

Remove stems from the mushrooms, saving them for other uses; cut the heads in quarters down through the tops; wash and leave drying on a paper towel.

Wash salad and leave drying on a paper towel; prepare the salad dressing.

Butter a baking dish, e.g., a cocotte; drain the water from the hominy and put it in the buttered dish; dot the top liberally with butter.

Cooking ***35 minutes***

Start the oven to bring it to 350°. Put the hominy in the warming oven.

30 minutes

Fry the chicken pieces in 2 cubic inches of butter, insides down first, then outsides till they are the brown you want them to be when served; salt and pepper. (This frying should take no more than five minutes.) Lay them in a baking dish and put them in the 350° oven to cook through.

Reducing the heat under the frying pan, gently fry the chopped shallots in the remaining fat without allowing them to brown; the pan should be brown (glazed) from frying the chicken. Add ½ cup of white wine; boil, briskly scraping the pan's bottom with a wooden spoon to release the glaze into the wine; in this process the wine should reduce by about half its volume. Add half a can of beef consommé (five ounces), the juice of half a lemon, and the quartered mushroom heads; leave the mixture simmering over the lowest heat to reduce into the sauce. With it complete save for the finishing touches you should have at least ten minutes free to greet your guest and to have a cocktail. But keep an eye on the simmering sauce and on the chicken and the hominy in the oven to be sure that they are not cooking too fast.

5 minutes

Remove the chicken pieces from the oven, arrange them on the platter on which you wish to serve them, keeping them warm in the oven with its door open; pour into the sauce in the frying pan any juice that has accumulated in the baking dish; add 2 cubic inches of butter to the sauce (butter is its real substance, flavored by the other components); remove the quartered mushroom heads with a perforated spoon and arrange them around the chicken pieces on the platter; add the chopped parsley to the sauce, pouring some of it over the chicken pieces and putting the rest in a bowl to serve apart. Serve the hominy in its baking dish.

If you wish to extend this meal, a good preliminary would be a cream of celery soup. Fruit would be an adequate and appropriate dessert.

Chicken Bercy may be served with either red or white wine.

Menu 2

Pork Chops   Applesauce

Dinner for two

An elegant meal of supposedly humble ingredients.

Shopping list

2 thick pork chops, at their best when the lean meat is marked by striations of fat.

2 lbs. of red-skinned apples, preferably tart cooking apples.

Salad, as you will.

Preparations

Wash and dry the salad: prepare the salad dressing.

Chop enough parsley to yield a tablespoonful and with a fork blend it into 1 cubic inch of butter.

Cooking

60 minutes

Start the oven to bring it to 300°. In just enough butter to grease a frying pan initially so that the chops will not stick to it, fry the pork chops over medium heat till they are lightly browned; salt, pepper, and sprinkle over them ¼ teaspoonful of thyme. Removing the fry pan's handle, stand the chops in it on their bony side; if they are thick, they will stand by themselves; if not, they can be kept standing by piercing them with a spit, the ends of which rest on the pan's sides. Put the chops in the 300° oven for long, slow cooking.

50 minutes

Cut the apples lengthwise into quarters and put them to boil—cores, skins, and all—in ½ cup of water in a covered saucepan.

40 minutes

Purée them after ten minutes' boiling through the Foley Food Mill, which will eliminate seeds, tough cores, and some of the skin: the resulting purée should be smooth and pink from the skins. Season with lemon juice and if you must with sugar; but remember that apples in this meal are a vegetable, not a sweet apple "sauce." Keep the purée warm in a double boiler after boiling it a bit more if it happens to be too runny. Again, keeping an eye on the chops in the oven to be sure they are not cooking fast enough to burn, you are free for odd jobs and cocktails until you wish to serve.

5 minutes

Warm a serving platter in the oven; pour on it the applesauce, and lay the chops on it, putting on each half of the parsley butter, at the last moment so that the butter is still solid when you serve.

If you wish to extend this meal, canned tomato bouillon, garnished with a slice of lemon, would be a suitable preliminary. Cheese would be an adequate dessert. Pork chops should be served with red wine.

Menu 3

Sole Banaro Baked Bananas

Dinner for two

AN EASY way to cook an excellent fish, with an unusual vegetable and a fine sauce.

Shopping list

2 filets of lemon sole; if you cannot get lemon sole, gray sole is the next best, and failing that, enough of the smaller filets of flounder for two.

½ lb. of almonds in the shell, or ¼ lb. of raw shelled almonds.

2 lbs. of bananas.

Salad, as you will.

Preparations

Shell the almonds, boil them in their skins three minutes in water, and pop off the skins with your fingers. Slice the almonds lengthwise three or four times into long slivers. Cook them slowly in 3 cubic inches of butter, stirring constantly, until the almonds and the butter are a golden brown: this is Sauce Amandine. Season to taste with lemon juice and set aside for later use.

Butter a baking dish. Peel the bananas, and cut them in halves, lengthwise; arrange these pieces in the buttered baking dish; sprinkle them with the juice of a whole lemon and 1 teaspoonful of salt; dot them with small pieces from 1 cubic inch of butter.

Wash the filets of sole in running cold water and dry them on paper towels. Cut each filet lengthwise twice along its center strip to eliminate the strip: often it contains tiny bone ends (you can feel them with your fingers) and you can well afford to throw away this strip, no wider than a quarter inch. If the filets are those of lemon or gray sole, cut the resulting pieces in two, crosswise, as for this dish you want relatively small pieces.

Wash the salad; prepare the salad dressing.

Cooking

30 minutes

Start the oven to bring it to 350°. Put in a baking pan big enough to hold the pieces of sole 1 cubic inch of butter and put the pan in the warming oven to melt the butter. While it is melting, put ½ cup of bread crumbs on a piece of waxed paper and season them with 1 teaspoonful of salt and five grinds on the pepper grinder. When the butter in the pan is melted, remove it from the oven, and rub each piece of sole into the melted butter so that each is thoroughly buttered on both sides and edges. Roll the pieces in the seasoned breadcrumbs till no more will stick to them, and arrange them in the still-buttery pan.

20 minutes

Put the fish and the bananas into the 350° oven. Again you are free till serving, looking from time to time at the fish and bananas to be sure they are cooking at the proper speed: the finished fish should be the golden brown of "fried sole," the bananas a golden yellow, with a fleck or two of brown.

5 minutes

Warm the Sauce Amandine over low heat and serve in a sauce bowl apart. The fish and the bananas are served in the baking dishes.

A good preliminary for this meal would be oysters on the half shell, as you can now usually buy them from your fish shop when they are in season (see pp. 142 to 143); or when they are not in season, shrimps in Sauce Rémoulade (see p. 157). If you really want to extend this meal and yourself, why not finish it off with a small *omelette flambée* (see p. 192)?

It would then be a meal that calls for a well-chilled white wine throughout.

Menu 4

Veal in Cream Spinach

Dinner for two

VEAL as you may remember it from some fine French restaurant.

Shopping list

½ lb. of veal scaloppini, the thin slices of clear meat that are best bought at Italian butchers'; elsewhere they are sometimes called "veal birds" from another use for them; the point is to get thin slices of clear meat without fat or gristle.

1 package of frozen chopped spinach.

½ lb. of mushrooms.

Salad, as you will.

Be sure you have ½ cup of cream, preferably sour.

Preparations

Wash salad; prepare the salad dressing.

Remove the stems from the mushroom heads (saving the stems as always for other uses, e.g., duxelles, see p. 161); slice the heads crosswise in ⅛-inch slices; wash and leave drying on a paper towel.

Bring to a boil in a saucepan an ample quantity of salted water, and boil in it the frozen spinach till it is thawed out but still bright green; strain off the water and leave the blanched spinach draining in the sieve.

Cooking ***30 minutes***

Put ½ can of beef consommé to boil in the top of a double boiler directly on the flame to reduce it to a thick glaze, watching it constantly to see when it reaches this point, at which add to it 1 cubic inch of butter. Then put the double boiler top into its bottom over hot water. Start the oven to bring it to 300°.

25 minutes

Fry the pieces of veal in 1 cubic inch of butter in a fry pan; fry the first pieces till they are merely white and set them aside in a baking dish; as their juice has mixed with the butter, a brown glaze will have begun to form on the frying pan's bottom, which will augment as you fry the other pieces; you can give them a fine brown without overcooking them by rubbing them gently in the glaze as they fry; as they attain it set them aside in the baking dish and return the first white pieces briefly to the pan for their final coloration. Put all the pieces in the 300° oven to cook through.

Put the mushroom slices in the remaining butter in the frying pan; salt and pepper them; cook over a low heat. They will yield enough juice so that with a wooden spoon you can begin to deglaze the pan.

20 minutes

To remove any remaining moisture from the spinach, shake it in the sieve, and when it is as dry as you can get it, stir it into the reduced consommé and butter in the double boiler top and leave it there to cook gently; salt, and for my taste, add not more—perhaps less—than ¼ teaspoonful of grated nutmeg.

15 minutes

Finally deglaze the frying pan by adding ¼ cup of white wine, and by releasing any glaze that remains on the pan's bottom into the wine by scraping it off with a wooden spoon. Leave simmering to reduce the wine by about half its volume.

10 minutes

Add to the reduced wine ½ cup of cream, preferably sour, stirring it in well as you add it to produce an understandably creamy sauce. You are now free for a cocktail for ten minutes, or longer, if you choose to delay serving, and if you, at this point, turn off the oven and keep the cream sauce for the veal at the lowest simmer.

To serve, arrange the pieces of veal on a serving platter, pouring off into the cream sauce any juice that has accumulated in the baking pan. With a perforated spoon remove the mushroom slices from the sauce and arrange them over the pieces of veal. Pour over them part of the remaining cream sauce and serve the rest in a bowl. Serve the spinach in a vegetable dish.

An appropriate preliminary for this meal would be a few slices of smoked salmon freshly sliced off by your delicatessen man, served with buttered pumpernickel and lemon wedges. An agreeable dessert would be pineapple pieces or slices, preferably, of course, fresh, but admissibly the canned fruit drained of its juice, in either case "refreshed" with some liqueur, best the Swiss cherry brandy, kirsch.

With veal in cream sauce you should serve a white wine, which need not be too dry.

Menu 5

Scallops Meunière ***French Peas***

Luncheon (or dinner) for two

A WAY of cooking scallops which brings them to their best.

Shopping list

½ lb. of small or "bay" scallops: nothing else will be as good in this dish; the large or "sea" scallops are a poor alternative.

1 can of tiny peas, now available in a number of brands.

½ lb. of small white onions.

Salad, as you will.

Preparations

Wash and dry the salad; prepare the salad dressing.

Chop enough parsley to yield a tablespoonful.

Into a saucepan drain off the liquid from the can of peas; add ½ teaspoonful of salt, five grinds on the pepper grinder, 5 stalks of parsley tied in a piece of string to facilitate their later removal, and the peeled onions; simmer covered for ten minutes till the liquid is almost gone and the onions are nearly cooked. Remove the parsley and add 1 cubic inch of butter.

Cooking ***10 minutes***

In 1 cubic inch of butter simmer the scallops over moderate heat. They will not fry, but will release their juice to make a whitish liquid.

Continue to simmer until this liquid again becomes buttery, as it will in about ten minutes.

5 minutes

Put the peas without their liquid with the onions in the saucepan and warm over a moderate heat; don't boil. While watching them and the scallops, prepare 4 slices of toast.

To finish the scallops, add a dash of red pepper, the juice of half a lemon, enough to deglaze the pan, and finally the chopped parsley; if there seems not to be enough sauce, add another cubic inch of butter. In the end, the scallops should be tiny, gilded yellow with the sauce, which should be clear, and essentially buttery. Mound them on slices of toast, and serve on a platter, pouring over each mound whatever sauce remains in the pan—to the last drop! Serve the peas in a vegetable dish.

As indicated, this is a meal which requires last-minute cooking, but so little of it that, with the preparations called for, you can be excused for a final ten minutes while your guest has a final cocktail.

Traditionally, scallops are somehow in themselves the beginning of a meal; hence this menu admits no preliminary dish. If you feel it needs extending, extend it into dessert. A likely possibility would be stewed pears, which you have prepared from the finest fruit in the market (see p. 186); or even the finest preserved pears from a can.

This meal requires a white wine.

Menu 6

Hors d'oeuvres   Mushrooms Matinale

Luncheon for two

A PLEASANT meal for Saturday or Sunday noon, to precede a matinee, a concert, or simply an afternoon of conversation.

Shopping list

1 can of anchovy filets, flat, or rolled around a caper.
¼ lb. of bologna sausage, or liverwurst, as you prefer.

1 bunch of celery.

1 jar of a good American pickle, mustard pickles, "bread-and-butter" pickles, or what you will.

1 lb. of the finest whitest mushrooms you can find: the name of this dish, literally *morning mushrooms*, implies that the mushrooms you use in it were picked with the dew on them.

2 lbs. of tomatoes.

1 can of brown bread (the kind that goes with New England baked beans).

Preparations

Strip off the outer stalks of the bunch of celery (saving them for other uses, e.g., cream of celery soup, see p. 146). Cut the tender inner stalks crosswise into ⅛-inch slices, and mix them into mayonnaise.

If, as is quite feasible, you are doing all this well in advance, say just after breakfast, you will arrange your hors d'oeuvres on the platter on which you will serve them and keep it, well arranged, in the refrigerator till the moment of serving: arrange this celery mayonnaise, the sausage, the pickles, and the anchovy filets in a way that pleases you, and leave it in the refrigerator.

Remove the stems from the mushrooms (keeping them for other uses), wash the caps, and dry them on a paper towel.

Bring a saucepan of water to a boil, and immerse each tomato in the boiling water for a slow count of ten (seconds); when the tomatoes have cooled (i.e., when the skin has been cooked), you will find that the skin comes off easily when peeled with a knife. When you have peeled the tomatoes, cut them in quarters, and under running cold water, with your fingers wash out the seeds; the more you mangle them in the process, the better; put them aside on a plate for later use.

Cooking **20 minutes**

Fry the mushroom heads in 1 cubic inch of butter, tops up, for two minutes, then bottoms up for two minutes, salting and peppering them at this stage so that the salt will draw their juice. Pour over them the mangled deseeded tomatoes, add ¼ cup of marsala or sherry, and ½ can of beef consommé (five ounces). Leave this mixture simmering.

5 minutes

Fry 4 (or 6) ½-inch slices of brown bread in ½ cubic inch of butter, arrange them on a serving platter, and keep them and the platter warm in the lowest possible oven heat.

As you sit down to eat the hors d'oeuvres, add to the mushrooms at least ½ cup of cream, preferably sour. By this time the mangled tomatoes, wine, and consommé should have cooked down to a paste, and the addition of the cream will turn it into a reddish-brown creamy sauce. Leave simmering till you are ready for it. Serve on the brown bread slices.

In using brown bread instead of the French pastry shell, *vol au vent*, this is an American adaptation of a classic French dish. If you want to be more elegant, and are near a French bakery that supplies *vols au vent*, you can easily do it in the classic version: merely set the *vols au vent* to warm in an oven at its lowest possible heat. To my palate, the use of American brown bread is a distinct gustatory improvement: its flavor is somehow a peculiarly happy foil for this sauce.

This meal includes the preliminary course. If you want to extend it into a leisurely afternoon, try a dessert over which you can linger, say two or more cheeses, some fine pears, and a bowl of mixed nuts which are fun to crack and pick out. Somehow a luncheon beginning with hors d'oeuvres like these calls for no salad.

For the hors d'oeuvres and the mushrooms a white wine is indicated. With this leisurely dessert you might well also have a bottle of some dessert wine—port, madeira, or marsala.

Menu 7

Turkish Swordfish *Cooked Cucumbers*

Dinner for two

A COMMON fish made more delicious by good cookery, with a common vegetable cooked in an unusual way. This recipe is derived from an admirable pamphlet, *Turkish Recipes*, issued by the Turkish

Information Office in New York. In its original form it, like the following recipe, calls for spits. If you have not been able to buy or make them, don't be deterred from trying these two menus; if you lack them, you can simply broil the swordfish or lamb pieces on your broiler rack, turning them with a spatula.

Shopping list

1 lb. swordfish in a slice 1 inch thick, preferably fresh, but you will often have to buy it frozen; one of the happy characteristics of this recipe is that it makes even frozen swordfish taste better.

3 cucumbers.

Bacon: you will use only two long slices.

Salad, as you will.

Preparations

If the swordfish is still frozen, set it in a warm place to thaw, or even, if you are pressed for time, in a pan of warm water.

Through your finest grater grate an onion into a small bowl; strain the grated onion through a fine sieve into a medium-sized bowl to produce onion juice; throw the rest away: it has served its purpose. Add to the onion juice a dash of paprika, the juice of half a lemon, a tablespoonful of oil, ½ teaspoonful of salt, crumbled bay leaves, more or less as you like their flavor. (Our Turkish friends use more.)

Peel the cucumbers and slice them into ⅛-inch slices crosswise. Spread them on a platter; scatter over them a teaspoonful of salt, mixing it into them with your fingers. Leave them to give up their water, as they will under the influence of the salt.

Chop enough parsley to yield 1 tablespoonful.

Wash and dry the salad; prepare the salad dressing.

As soon as the swordfish is thawed, cut it into inch-square pieces, discarding any skin and brown fat. Dry the pieces in a paper towel. Emulsify the mixture in the bowl, as you emulsify a French salad dressing, and stir into it the swordfish pieces. They should remain in it at least half an hour, better an hour.

Slice into quarter-inch squares two long pieces of bacon.

Cooking *30 minutes*

Fry the bacon squares in a saucepan until they are tiny and crisp. Pour on them the sliced cucumbers and their water, adding 1 teaspoonful of sugar, 2 tablespoonfuls of tarragon vinegar, and five turns on the pepper grinder. Leave simmering.

15 minutes

Start the broiler. Push the swordfish pieces on two spits, or arrange them on the broiler rack.

10 minutes

Put the swordfish three inches under the broiler flame, turning them once or more as they brown.

5 minutes

Sprinkle over the simmering cucumbers 1 tablespoonful of flour and stir it in, to thicken their juice slightly. Melt 1 cubic inch of butter and, off the heat, add to it the chopped parsley.

To serve, put the swordfish pieces, on or off the spits, on a platter and pour over them the melted butter and parsley. Serve the cucumbers in a vegetable dish.

This menu somehow needs no preliminary. If you want to extend it, cold meat with the salad course is an agreeable possibility, say some very thinly sliced Italian ham, prosciutto, or Italian spiced beef, pastrami. Stewed kumquats, if they are in season, would contrast pleasantly as a dessert (see p. 188).

Swordfish calls for a dry white wine.

Menu 8

Shish Kebab   Pilaf

Dinner for two

ANOTHER Near Eastern dish, simple to prepare, delicious to consume: *shish*, spit; *kebab*, lamb.

Shopping list

½ lb. (or more if you are hearty) of lean lamb without fat or gristle. See first if you can persuade your butcher to produce it for you in regular 1-inch cubes. If you can't you can produce it for yourself by buying 1 lb. (or more) of the least expensive lamb chops and cutting out the kernels of lean meat. In preparing this dish for more than two, the best source of the meat is the thigh section of a leg of lamb which can now often be bought separately.

1 small packet of pine nuts, or pignolias, to be found in most Italian shops, often elsewhere.

1 lb. of green peas. (Frozen peas will do quite as well, except that you will not use an entire package.)

Preparations

Through your finest grater grate an onion into a small bowl; strain the grated onion through a fine sieve into a medium-sized bowl to produce onion juice. Add to the onion juice 2 tablespoonfuls of oil, ½ teaspoonful of salt, five grinds of the pepper grinder, ¼ teaspoonful each of thyme and marjoram, and a bay leaf if you like its flavor. Emulsify as you emulsify a French salad dressing and stir in the pieces of lamb. Let them remain in this dressing at least half an hour, better an hour.

Wash and dry the salad; prepare the salad dressing.

If the peas are fresh, shell them.

Cooking

Start the oven to bring it to 350°. ***40 minutes***

35 minutes

Put 2 cubic inches of butter in a saucepan and over gentle heat fry in it the pignolias, approximately 2 tablespoonfuls of them. Stir them constantly so that they turn an even gold without browning. To the butter and nuts add ½ cup of rice, stirring it in the butter over still gentle heat till the grains are thoroughly coated with butter and turn transparent. (A variation at this point which some like, but which is unorthodox in the Near East, is to allow the butter and the rice to brown a bit.) Add to the buttered rice 1 cup of liquid, merely water, or for more flavor ½ cup of water and ½ cup of some meat stock, e.g., beef consommé. Add the peas, no more than a quarter package if frozen peas are used. Bring the mixture to a boil and pour into a cocotte; set it to cook in the 350° oven.

15 minutes

Start the broiler. Push the pieces of lamb on two spits.

10 minutes

Check the progress of the pilaf in the oven; by this time the pilaf will have partly thickened, and the peas and pignolias will have risen to its top; stir them back into the pilaf with a two-tined fork.

5 minutes

Put the lamb on the spits as close to the broiler flame as you can without their catching fire; turn once or more during this rapid cooking; when finished, as they should be in five minutes, unless you insist on having your lamb cooked dry and gray, they should be dark brown outside, even with flecks of burned meat, and pink at the center. Remember that meat on spits cooks more quickly because the metal of the spit carries heat to its center.

To serve, pour the pilaf, which should by now be devoid of liquid, with each grain of rice separate from the others, on a platter. Lay the lamb on its spits on the rice, to be removed at the table with a two-tined fork run down the spit.

To extend this menu, the classic preliminary for me is the cabbage borscht served before it in a fine Turkish restaurant such as Karpich's at Ankara; it can now be bought in the United States in cans. A most appropriate dessert, Ottoman in spirit, would be fine canned apricots in their juice sprinkled with slivers of raw almond.

Shish kebab calls for a red wine.

There are, of course, many variations of both dishes on this menu. Some of our Turkish friends who prefer their kebab rare use the green twigs of some bush for spits; one of them in New York once cooked kebab for me on bamboo plant sticks which he had sandpapered to remove the green paint that colors them. The classic shish kebab is only lamb, but it may be garnished with whole small tomatoes, with mushroom heads, or even with squares of bacon between the pieces of lamb.

The basic rule for pilaf is that implicit in this menu: rice, fried in different greases, cooked slowly in twice its volume of some liquid. Chopped onions can replace the pignolias in the first stage; raisins, preferably those made from tiny currants, can replace the peas in the second stage. A particularly delicious variation is to substitute for the rice the cracked wheat that can be found in shops specializing in oriental foods.

Finally, shish kebab is an excellent dish for outdoor cooking: at its best in Turkey it is cooked over charcoal brought to its most intense heat by fanning it.

Menu 9

Antipasto Spaghetti

Dinner for two

THE BEGINNING of an Italian meal, but for most Americans nearly a meal in itself.

Shopping list

Your shopping for this meal will be simplified by your seeking out some Italian grocery where all of its ingredients can readily be found.

½ pound of spaghetti, preferably the thin spaghetti known as "spaghettini, No. 2."

1 can (approximately a pound) of Italian (plum) tomatoes put up by some producer with an Italian name; apart from being packed with some basil in them, tomatoes of this type do seem better for this purpose.

A small bunch of fresh basil if it is in season; if not, dried basil.

½ pint of ripe olives, best the kind that are preserved in oil: most Italian stores have a number of varieties.

1 can of anchovy filets.

1 small can of eggplant appetizer, in Italian known as *Caponata.*

¼ lb. of hard salami, sliced as thin as possible.

½ lb. of grated spaghetti cheese.

1 lb. of ricotta, the fresh Italian "cottage" cheese.

½ lb. of fresh mushrooms.

Salad, as you will.

Be sure you have tomato paste on hand.

Preparations

Break out the mushroom stems, wash and dry the heads, and cut them crosswise into ⅛-inch slices. Peel and grate 1 medium-sized onion through your medium grater. Peel and crush 2 cloves of garlic and fry them in 2 cubic inches of butter, stirring them constantly till they are golden, but without browning them or the butter; if you prefer, olive oil (4 tablespoonfuls) may be substituted for the butter, or you may use a mixture of butter and oil (1 cubic inch of butter and 2 tablespoonfuls of oil). Remove the garlic, add the grated onion, and fry till it is golden but not browned, again stirring constantly. Stir in the mushroom slices, add 2 teaspoonfuls of salt and ten grinds on the pepper grinder. When the mushroom slices have yielded their juice under the influence of the salt, stir into the mixture a full can of tomato paste, and let the mixture simmer over low heat, stirring it occasionally, until it ceases to steam, it exudes its oil or butter, and the originally bright red of the paste has turned a mahogany color. To my mind this is the most important phase of making a spaghetti sauce, and the phase in which its basic flavor is established; it may require twenty minutes of occasional stirring and close watching but is well worth it in the outcome. During it, wash and chop enough parsley and fresh basil to yield 2 tablespoonfuls of each (if dried basil is used, 1 tablespoonful will suffice); open the canned Italian tomatoes, and when the basis of the sauce is ready, add them, the parsley, and the basil to the mixture. Simmer the resulting sauce for at least an hour, covered so that it will not spatter, adding water in small quantities as may be necessary to produce a sauce of the consistency you prefer. This is a sauce which keeps well, and if, as I often do, you make it well in advance of your meal, bottle it off in Ball jars and refrigerate.

Not too far in advance of the meal arrange the antipastos on plates: usually each person's share of the eggplant appears on the plate's center, with the anchovies, salami, and the ripe olives arranged around it, or, for example, with the anchovy filets laid across it.

Cooking ***20 minutes***

Start heating to a boil a large saucepan of water; start warming, preferably in a double boiler, as much of the spaghetti sauce as will be needed. Wash and dry the salad; prepare the salad dressing.

10 minutes

Put ½ lb. of spaghetti into the now-boiling water, stirring the stiff pieces into a circular pattern as they soften but trying not to break them so that they can be served in their original length. True amateurs of spaghetti prefer it what some might think a trifle tough, *al dente*, as the amateurs say; a boiling of about nine minutes is right for my taste. At this point drain the spaghetti in a colander, and while it is draining, melt 2 cubic inches of butter in the saucepan in which the spaghetti was boiled; when the butter is melted and the spaghetti is fully drained, return it to the saucepan and thoroughly stir the melted butter into it. Keep it warm, as, for example, in the oven at the lowest possible heat, while you are eating the antipastos.

Spaghetti is best served on a platter or round serving plate, if you wish, with a little sauce poured over the center as a kind of garnish, but with the rest served apart in a bowl; thus you may take as much as you want of each. Also serve apart in a bowl the grated spaghetti cheese. Though some assert it to be vulgar, I prefer to eat spaghetti with a soupspoon in my left hand, a fork in my right, winding the long pieces on the fork with its tines revolving almost vertically in the spoon's bowl.

A most appropriate dessert for this meal is the Italian "cottage" cheese, ricotta, included in the shopping list. Lighter than the usual cottage cheese, it is delicious eaten by itself as ice cream is eaten. Or it may be eaten sprinkled with granulated sugar, or cinnamon, or a mixture of the two.

The traditional wine for this meal is a red chianti, Italian or American.

Menu 10

Curry of Chicken Indian Rice

Dinner for two

An admittedly Western version of an oriental dish, but one of the best, and the most readily prepared, of the number I have tried.

Shopping list

2 breast pieces of chicken, or enough to yield four single breasts and four wings.

3 large bananas.

1 tart cooking apple.

1 small can of shredded coconut.

1 small can of ripe olives.

1 small jar of curry powder. The Indian curry powders which now can be found in specialty shops are distinctly superior to most put up by Western packers.

1 small jar of chutney.

½ lb. of salted peanuts.

Salad, as you will.

Preparations

Boil the chicken pieces in water, or, for more flavor, in diluted chicken consommé for thirty minutes. Pour off the broth unless you have some other early use for it, and when the pieces have cooled, remove the white meat from its skin and bones in as solid pieces as you can: the individual breasts, for example, should come off in two pieces, what the French call the major and the minor filets. If you are preparing the chicken meat well in advance, it can be kept moist by putting the pieces in the refrigerator in a closed container with 2 tablespoonfuls of the broth.

To prepare the curry sauce, grate 2 medium-sized onions through the medium grater and start them frying in 1 cubic inch of butter in a saucepan, not allowing them to brown. Meanwhile, peel, core, and slice the tart apple, peel and slice crosswise 1 banana, measure out ¼ cup of shredded coconut, and start them cooking with the onions. With lengthwise cuts, slice the meat from 6 ripe olives, measure out ¼ cup of raisins, and add them to the mixture. Stir 2 tablespoonfuls of curry powder into 1 cup of milk, eliminating any lumps in stirring, and add. Further season the sauce with 2 teaspoonfuls of salt, ten grinds on the pepper grinder, and 1 teaspoonful of chopped tarragon if you can procure it; if not, 1 tablespoonful of tarragon vinegar. Let the sauce simmer at least an hour, adding milk in small quantities as necessary for the consistency you want—it should be relatively stiff and not runny. If you are preparing this sauce well in advance—and it will be the better for sitting a bit—refrigerate it until you use it.

Cooking

30 minutes

Start water to boil in a large saucepan with 2 teaspoonfuls of salt. Start to warm in a double boiler as much of the curry sauce as you want to use, again correcting its consistency, when it is warm, by adding milk if necessary.

Boil in the salted water 1 cup of rice.

25 minutes

Wash and dry the salad; make the salad dressing. Put the remaining shredded coconut, the salted peanuts, the chutney, and the remaining 2 bananas, peeled and sliced crossways, in bowls, preferably similar, to go on the four corners of the table as the four "corner pieces" traditional with this curry.

15 minutes

Start the oven to bring it to 350°. Drain the rice from its cooking water in a colander, and set the rice, which should by now be cooked soft and, in some varieties, fluffy, under running cold water to wash off any clinging starch.

10 minutes

Drain the washed rice in the colander, pour it into a cocotte, and put in the 350° oven to warm and dry.

5 minutes

Fry the chicken pieces (drained of any broth if you refrigerated them in it) in 1 cubic inch of butter, not to brown, but merely to warm them in it.

To serve the curry, pour the sauce on a platter or round serving dish, and arrange the pieces of chicken at its center, pouring over them any butter remaining in the frying pan. Serve the rice in its cocotte, stirring it with a two-tined fork to emphasize its fluffiness. The curry and rice are eaten with the components of the four corner dishes.

An appropriate preliminary to this meal (and its components can readily be kept warm while a preliminary is eaten) would be some fine Scandinavian herring in white wine, such as can be found in specialty shops. For dessert, some tropical fruit would be ideal: mangoes, for example.

For me, a curry calls for a well-chilled dry white wine.

Leftover chicken curry, puréed through the Foley Food Mill, further diluted with whole milk and thoroughly chilled, makes a delectable hot-weather soup (see p. 149).

Conversation piece: I originally had this recipe for curry from a Boston architect, long since dead, who enlivened the serving of it with an account, supposedly authentic, of how he acquired it. During World War I he was involved in counterespionage, and in his work encountered a captured spy who came to be known to him as Bob Rabbett. Professionally attracted to him, my architect friend called on him the day before he was to be executed at dawn, to ask if there were any dish he particularly craved for his last meal. Rabbett replied that he would die relatively happy if he could have for that meal a curry of which he was particularly fond. This is the recipe for Bob Rabbett's curry! If, in serving it, you are tempted to recount this anecdote, it is well to terminate its telling with an *absit omen.*

Menu 11

Lamb Chops   Purée of Peas

Dinner for two

THE FIRST of a series of five menus presenting meats frequently served—but with a difference.

Shopping list

2, or if you are hearty, 4 lamb chops, at least an inch thick.
2 packages of frozen peas.
Salad, as you will.

Preparations

Wash and dry the salad; prepare the salad dressing.

Wash and chop enough parsley to yield 1 tablespoonful, and with a fork blend it into 1 cubic inch of butter.

Prepare the lamb chops: if they are from that part of the ribs that yields long tails, remove the extra, central fat, roll the tails inward, and skewer them with a wooden toothpick; in any case, rub each side of each chop with a clove of garlic cut in half and grate a bit on the rough chop bone; pepper each side with two turns on the pepper grinder; rub into each side approximately ½ teaspoonful of oil.

Cooking

20 minutes

Start to boil a saucepan full of water salted with 2 teaspoonfuls of salt.

15 minutes

Start the broiler. Put into the boiling, salted water the two packages of frozen peas.

10 minutes

Put the chops into the preheated broiler as close as you can to the flame without their catching fire.

5 minutes

Turn the chops. Drain off the water from the still green peas through the Foley Food Mill: purée them into the saucepan in which they boiled, adding 1 cubic inch of butter, and return them briefly to low heat to melt the butter and to dry.

Serve the chops on a preheated platter with a share of the parsley and butter on each and the purée of peas in a neat mound on either end of the platter.

As a preliminary to this menu, a cream of mushroom soup would do well, and as a dessert, baked apples *bonne femme*. (See pp. 145 and 188, respectively.)

Throughout a red wine of the claret type is called for.

Menu 12

Steak *Baked Potatoes*

Dinner for two

A TRADITIONAL meal with unusual touches.

Shopping list

The smallest, thickest steak your butcher can supply: ask him for that, and put him on his mettle; in New York, he might respond with the "first cut of the sirloin," called in New England "the first cut of the rump"; tell him it is for a special occasion, and persuade him, if you can, to cut it for you from a well-aged quarter hanging in his refrigerator. In general, really prime steak is dark red in color, with striations of white fat in the lean meat. If you can't get the butcher to respond to this challenge, settle for two 1½-inch-thick slices of tenderloin: it will have less flavor, but you can otherwise rely on it.

3 small, well-shaped baking potatoes.

Salad, as you will.

Preparations

Wash and dry the salad; make the salad dressing.

Wash and chop enough parsley to yield 1 tablespoonful; with a fork blend it into 1 cubic inch of butter.

Pepper each side of the steak with five grinds from the pepper grinder, and rub each side with oil till the oil emulsifies with the meat and turns white.

Cooking ***60 minutes***

Wash the 3 baking potatoes and put them to bake in an oven set at 400°. For this menu you then have nothing but odd jobs for the next forty minutes.

Start the broiler. ***20 minutes***

15 minutes

Put the steak in the broiler as close to the flame as you can without its catching fire. Give it first three minutes of this intense heat on each side, then two minutes each. After these ten minutes of brisk cooking, leave it in the unlighted broiler to "rest."

10 minutes

Meanwhile, take out of the oven the by-now-baked potatoes; cut them neatly in half, lengthwise, holding them in a pot holder in your hand; still holding them so, scoop them out of the skins and purée them through the Foley Food Mill; add 1 cubic inch of butter, ½ teaspoonful of salt, five grinds on the pepper grinder, and replace the puréed potato in the skins. Melt ½ cubic inch of butter and brush the tops of the purée.

To serve, transfer the steak from the broiler to a preheated platter and keep warm. Relight the broiler, and expose to its flame the halved baked potatoes, quickly to brown their top surfaces. Arrange them around the steak on its platter. Dot the steak with the parsley butter, salt, and serve with the parsley butter unmelted but melting.

For a 1½-inch steak this procedure will produce a steak that is properly rare, brown to near burning outside, evenly graduated from both sides to real rareness in the middle. If you must have your steak better done, allow twenty minutes for broiling, five minutes for each side, twice.

A preliminary to this meal is a bit hard to arrange, since it requires timed cooking at the very end. If a preliminary is called for, you can manage it, both in preparation and in eating, with filets of anchovy neatly laid parallel on toast; you can join in eating them while the steak is resting and just before you must relight the broiler to brown the potatoes. For dessert, this somehow seems a meal for a sturdy blue cheese, a roquefort, or a gorgonzola, or a good Danish blue.

Steak likewise calls for a sturdy red wine.

A steak is "rested," i.e., kept in a warm place, such as the unlighted broiler of this menu, so that its brisk cooking from the outside can penetrate the inner meat. If a thick steak is not so "rested," it may be nearly burned outside and raw in the middle.

Menu 13

Roast Chicken Turnips

Dinner for two

ANOTHER traditional meal, easier to do in this version, and also with a difference.

Shopping list

1 small broiling chicken, the smallest you can buy, *not* split for broiling, but cleaned for roasting, with the neck bone cut out. If you are cooking this dinner for more than two, you will do better to get two or more of these small birds rather than one larger one.

2 lbs. of the small white turnips that are now almost always in vegetable shops; or, failing them, 2 lbs. of parsnips, which are prepared in precisely the same way.

Salad, as you will.

Preparations

Set 2 cubic inches of butter in a warm place to soften slightly. Wash the chicken inside and out and dry with paper towels. Turn the neck skin on the bird's back and secure it by locking it under the wings. Push down the legs, and with your trussing needle thread butcher's twine through both thighs and the body of the bird; still holding down the legs, push the needle with its twine back through the lower legs; tie the two ends of the twine tightly to hold the legs in this position while the bird roasts. With your hand rub into the bird's skin 1 cubic inch of the softened butter, particularly into the breast and legs. With your still-buttery hand butter the inside and cover of a saucepan with a removable handle that can be put in the oven. Put any surplus butter inside the bird. Put the bird in the pan; salt and pepper.

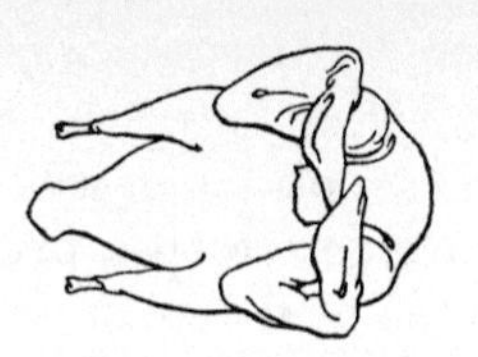

Chicken from the bottom: wings bent in to hold the skin of the neck.

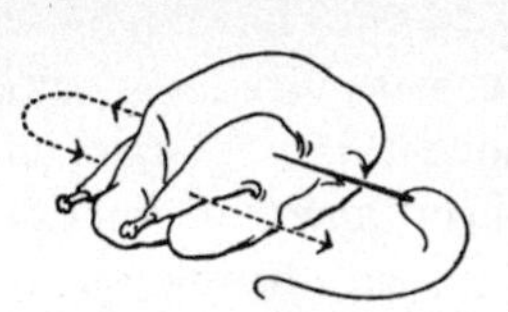

Trussing: needle and string through thighs and back through legs.

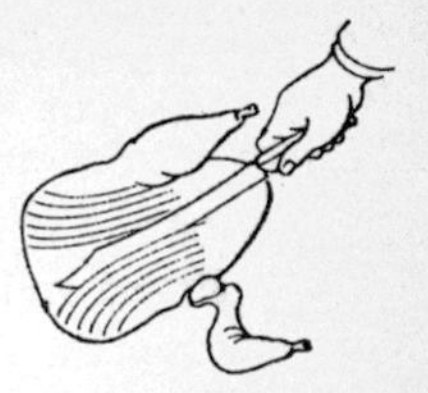

Carving.

Peel the turnips (or parsnips) and cut them into ¼-inch rounds. Blanch these slices by boiling them for five minutes in salted water. While they are boiling, melt in a cocotte 2 cubic inches of butter, as you can most readily by briefly starting the oven. Drain the sliced turnips and leave them to cool. Into the now-melted butter in the cocotte stir 1 tablespoonful of dry mustard and 2 tablespoonfuls of brown sugar. Work the sliced turnips into this sauce with your fingers, and when the turnips are thoroughly impregnated with it, arrange them in circular rows.

Wash and dry the salad; prepare the salad dressing.

Cooking

Start the oven to bring it to 350°. ***60 minutes***

50 minutes

Put the chicken in the 350° oven with the buttered cover on the pan.

30 minutes

Put the cocotte of turnips in the oven, taking the opportunity of looking at the roasting chicken; at this point it should scarcely be browning, but rather should look golden and steaming. Re-cover as quickly as possible.

20 minutes

Remove the cover from the pan in which the chicken is roasting to allow it to brown. To get a fine brown, you may need to increase the oven's heat (doing so will be equally good for the turnips).

5 minutes

Set a teaspoonful of arrowroot flour to soften briefly in ¼ cup of white wine. Remove the chicken from the pan (I find the soup skimmer the best tool for this operation: its right-angled spoon can gradually be slipped under the chicken, loosening it from the bottom of the pan, so that it can be lifted out without breaking); cut the trussing twine and remove it; put the chicken on the platter on which it is to be served and keep it warm, for example on the open oven door. Replacing the saucepan's handle, on the top of the stove over moderate heat work off the glaze that will have formed on the pan's bottom by adding 1 cup of consommé (beef or chicken) and stirring the glaze into it with a wooden spoon. Thicken the resulting liquid with the white wine and arrowroot flour. Straining the thickened sauce through a fine sieve, put one third of it over the chicken and the rest in a bowl to serve apart.

The turnips are served in the cocotte in which they baked. Traditionally, a roast chicken on its platter is garnished with water cress. A roast chicken is best carved first by cutting off each thigh at the thigh joint, then by thinly slicing the white meat of the breast; each guest can then choose the part he prefers.

A fine preliminary for this meal would be a cream of oyster soup (see p. 147). Brandied or jubilee cherries (see p. 187) would be a prime dessert.

If you prefer your roast chicken stuffed, stuff it with duxelles (see p. 161) which you have accumulated for this purpose, but allow sixty minutes rather than fifty for the roasting, as stuffed birds always require longer.

This meal may be accompanied by either a red or a white wine, as you prefer.

This way of roasting is the classic way: it yields a fine product, well browned, and retaining its own moisture, and a sauce that is *sui generis*. No tedious basting is called for, because it is a principle of classic roasting that no alien liquid intrudes.

Menu 14

Baked Ham Braised Endives

Dinner for two

A SIMPLE but classic dinner, involving a vegetable too seldom served as such in the United States.

Shopping list

1 slice of ham, at least ⅝-inch thick.
1 lb. of endive.
Salad, as you will.

Preparations

Make clear brown sauce (see p. 152).

Remove any discolored outside leaves from the endives, and cut any brown from their root end. Bring a pan of salted water to a boil and simmer the endives in it for five minutes; drain them in a colander. Butter a cocotte with 1 cubic inch of butter; arrange the endives in it; season with ½ teaspoonful of salt, five grinds on the pepper grinder, and the juice of half a lemon; sprinkle over them ¼ cup of beef consommé.

Butter a flat baking dish and lay in it the slice of ham.

Wash and dry the salad; make the salad dressing.

Cooking

Start the oven to bring it to 300°. ***35 minutes***

30 minutes

Put the ham and the endives in the 300° oven. The endives will take care of themselves, but you must turn the ham frequently, at least every five minutes, during the first fifteen minutes of its baking if you wish it to come out flat; until it is partly cooked, the greater heat of the pan on its bottom side will tend to make it curl.

15 minutes

Reheat the clear brown sauce, and add to it ¼ cup of seedless raisins, and leave it simmering over the lowest possible heat.

5 minutes

With a spoon spread 3 tablespoonfuls of the clear brown sauce over the endives which by now should be slightly browned, avoiding the raisins; finish the sauce with the raisins in it by adding ¼ cup of marsala or sherry.

Serve the ham on a platter with a little of the sauce poured over it and the rest in a bowl apart. Serve the endives in their cocotte.

A potage Parmentier (see p. 148) would make a fine preliminary to this meal. A refreshing dessert would be fresh orange sections. Peel the oranges as you would an apple, cutting just slightly into the meat; holding the peeled orange over a bowl to catch its juice, cut out the wedges of clear flesh between the membranes. The addition of a little curaçao or cointreau makes of this a rather elegant dessert.

This meal may be accompanied by either a light red or white wine.

If endives happen not to be on the market, you can substitute for them braised hearts of celery, prepared in almost precisely the same way: trim off all but the tiniest inner leaves; trim the root end; blanch in salted boiling water ten minutes rather than five.

Menu 15

Veal Chops Stuffed Tomatoes

Dinner for two

A WAY of cooking American veal, which makes it as tender as the European variety, with a handsome vegetable.

Shopping list

2 or 4 veal chops, depending on appetite and size; good-sized chops, corresponding to the sirloin in beef, are really preferable.

4 small, firm tomatoes, which now often come packed in boxes of four.

½ lb. of mushrooms (unless you have prepared and saved duxelles for this meal).

Salad, as you will.

Preparations

Make clear brown sauce (see p. 152), reserving ¼ cup of the can of beef consommé which it calls for for another use, and adding to it 1 tablespoonful of tomato paste, or, if you haven't a can open, 1 tablespoonful of ketchup.

Prepare duxelles from the mushroom stems, reserving the heads for some other use (see p. 161).

Butter a small baking dish. With an apple corer, remove the cores of the tomatoes from the stem side, to make a cylindrical hole to two thirds of their depth, being careful not to pierce the bottoms. Fill this hole with duxelles, mounding a little on the top. Arrange them in the buttered baking dish.

Chop enough parsley to yield 1 tablespoonful.

Wash and dry the salad; make the salad dressing.

Cooking

Start the oven to bring it to 300°. ***60 minutes***

50 minutes

On the shelf on a piece of waxed paper spread ½ cup of flour and sprinkle over it 1 teaspoonful of salt and ten grinds of the pepper grinder. Trim off any dangling tails from the chops; they add nothing and get in the way. Rub both sides of the chops in the flour till they are well coated. Fry them till their outsides are golden brown in 1 cubic inch of butter in a frying pan with a removable handle and for which you have a tight-fitting cover. Removing the handle, sprinkle over them the ¼ cup of consommé you reserved from the clear brown sauce; cover; and put in the 300° oven. This should allow the time they need for cooking.

30 minutes

Put the stuffed tomatoes in their baking dish in the 300° oven, taking the occasion to look briefly at the veal chops; they should be no browner but should simply be steaming in the consommé and their own juice. Re-cover them as quickly as possible.

5 minutes

Rewarm the clear brown tomato-flavored sauce. Remove the chops from the oven and arrange them on the platter on which they are to be served, keeping them warm; for example, on the open oven door. Deglaze the pan in which they have cooked with the clear brown sauce on the top of the stove over moderate heat. Through a fine sieve pour one third of it over the chops on their platter and serve the rest in a bowl apart. With a spatula remove the baked tomatoes and arrange them at the four corners of the platter. Sprinkle the chops and the tomatoes with the chopped parsley.

This is a meal for which a cream of corn soup (see p. 146) would be an agreeable preliminary and one which the cook can enjoy, since the chops and the tomatoes will not suffer from being kept warm while it is being enjoyed; indeed, sitting a bit gives the chops under their share of the sauce a finer glaze; if you are inclined to linger over soup, however, you would do well to delay sprinkling the parsley till just before you serve, so that it is bright green, to contrast with the mahogany brown of the glazed chops and the bright red of the baked tomatoes.

For a dessert, some fine stewed fruit would be in keeping (see p. 186.)

This meal calls for a light red wine.

Menu 16

Boiled Beef   Assorted Vegetables

Dinner for two

A TRADITIONAL American meal, New England boiled dinner, which now need not be difficult to prepare, and which, properly prepared, can be elegant.

Shopping list

2 lbs. of the finest corned beef your butcher can supply. Let him pick it out for you; but it should be a well-shaped piece, with fat on the outside and streaks of fat through it.

1 small (8¼ ounce) can of tiny carrots: these small cans of "tiny" vegetables come and go on the market; when I find them in stock, I buy up a supply.

1 small can of tiny beets.
1 small can of small onions.
1 small can of small boiled potatoes.
1 small green cabbage.
1 small bottle of grated horse-radish.

Preparations

This is a meal that centers in the long cooking of one component, the corned beef. It is also a meal which, with minimum advance preparations, leaves the cook free till the moment of serving. Assuming that you wish to be free till the last moment, the things you can do in advance are listed under this heading.

No salad is included in the shopping list, because this is a meal that seems to call for none.

Prepare horse-radish sauce for the boiled beef: simply mix 2 tablespoonfuls of grated horse radish with 2 tablespoonfuls of sour cream, refrigerate till you want it in the bowl in which you will serve it.

Open the 4 small cans of vegetables (carrots, beets, onions, and potatoes) and pour off the liquid; a simple way of draining them is not quite to cut out the top, to pour off what liquid pours out, and to leave them draining upside down in the sink. Melt 2 cubic inches of butter. Arrange the 4 vegetables each by itself in a baking dish, and pour over them the melted butter. Again, if you are doing this well in advance, refrigerate.

Cooking

3 hours

The long, slow cooking of the beef requires 3 hours. Fill a soup kettle three quarters full of water and add to it sliced crosswise an onion, a carrot, a stalk of celery if you have it (it's not essential), 5 stalks of parsley, ¼ teaspoonful of thyme, ¼ teaspoonful of marjoram, a bay leaf, and 12 peppercorns. Add the piece of corned beef, and simmer for the balance of three hours over the lowest heat that will keep it just at a gentle boil. Add water if necessary to keep the beef covered.

30 minutes

Start the oven to bring it to 300°. If you have refrigerated the vegetables, particularly if you have refrigerated them in a Pyrex baking dish, remove from the refrigerator at this time, because sometimes a chilled baking dish breaks on being put into even a moderate oven.

20 minutes

Peel off the outer leaves of the green cabbage and slice it lengthwise into four quarters; lay the sliced quarters on their sides and cut out lengthwise the tougher central portions, particularly toward the stem.

10 minutes

With the skimming spoon lift out the beef from its broth, drain it well, and put it on the center of the platter on which it will be served. Put the cabbage quarters into the still-simmering broth. Keep the beef warm.

To serve, garnish the beef on its platter with the cabbage quarters, which should be still bright green. Serve the other vegetables in their baking dish.

This is a homely meal that calls for no preliminary, as for no salad. An appropriate dessert would be a New England Indian pudding such as you can find well made in cans by Boston packers. The present New England way of serving it is with vanilla ice cream; it used to be served with sweetened whipped cream.

A light red wine goes well with this meal.

It is doubtful that two will eat 2 lbs. of corned beef; but while you are cooking it, you will do well to cook at least this quantity: sliced thin, cold, it is delicious with salad as a cold meat; ground through the meat grinder it becomes the staple of simple corned-beef hash, or, more important, of "red-flannel" hash (see p. 160). I am never sure whether I want a boiled dinner for itself, or for this latter hash, which is simply the same ingredients cooked in a different way.

Finally, don't feel pangs of conscience at simply pouring out the broth in which the beef and cabbage were cooked: there's really nothing you can do with it; it has served its purpose.

Menu 17

Pork Spareribs Red Cabbage

Dinner for two

AN AMERICAN classic, with a European accompaniment that suits it.

Shopping list

1 fresh pork sparerib, i.e., the rib bones from which most of the meat has been trimmed, now readily found in some butcher shops and in almost any shop that specializes in pork.
1 small red cabbage.
2 tart cooking apples.
Salad, as you will.

Preparations

Again, this is a meal that centers in the long cooking, this time, of two components. It is also a meal that leaves you virtually free until it is ready to serve, except that it requires periodic attention.

Make a "barbecue sauce" of the following ingredients: 2 cubic inches of butter, ½ cup of ordinary vinegar—cider or cheap red-wine vinegar, ½ can of tomato paste, the juice of a lemon, 1 teaspoonful of salt, ¼ teaspoonful of thyme, a bay leaf, and ten grinds on the pepper grinder. To "make" this sauce, simply warm the ingredients in a saucepan till the butter has melted.

Remove the outside leaves of the red cabbage; cut it in quarters lengthwise, and laying each quarter on its side cut out lengthwise the tougher central portions; slice the remaining cabbage, still lengthwise, into ¼-inch-wide shreds.

Wash and dry the salad; make the salad dressing.

Cooking *2 hours*

Start the oven to bring it to 300°. As it warms, lay the spareribs in a big baking pan, outer, convex side up, painting the barbecue sauce on it with a butter brush.

1 hour, 50 minutes

Put the spareribs in the 300° oven for long, slow cooking, turning it after twenty minutes, and painting the inner, concave side with the sauce; and so on, each twenty minutes; this may seem a chore, but the result makes it worth your while: apparently the principle is that by such cooking and basting the fat of the pork is tried out and replaced by the sauce.

1 hour

In a heavy saucepan, melt 2 cubic inches of butter, and stir into it the shredded red cabbage; cover, and let it simmer in the butter and its juice, stirring occasionally.

50 minutes

Peel, core and slice into ¼-inch slices the 2 cooking apples; add them to the cabbage, together with ¼ cup of red wine vinegar (or ¼ cup of red wine), 1 teaspoonful of salt, ten grinds from the pepper grinder, and ten grates of nutmeg on the nutmeg grater (¼ teaspoonful). Leave simmering on the lowest possible heat.

Serve the spareribs, convex side up, on a platter: to carve, you cut between every two or three ribs with a sharp, sturdy knife. Serve the red cabbage in a vegetable dish.

Since neither of these dishes requires any last-minute attention save oversight, the cook is free to enjoy a preliminary, say a cream of shrimp soup (see p. 146). For dessert after these rich dishes, some berries—strawberries, raspberries, even blueberries—fresh, if in season, stewed otherwise, would be appropriate.

This meal calls for a red wine.

I owe this recipe and an understanding of its underlying principle —the replacement of the fat by the sauce—to our painter friend, Maurice Grosser, who in his delightful book, *Painting in Public*, remarked, "Painting and cooking are very much alike."

Menu 18

Oxtail Soup Fondue

Supper (or luncheon) for two

A MEAL which, with advance preparation, can be ready as soon as you are ready for it.

Shopping list

1 oxtail: get the butcher to cut it into 1-inch-thick pieces crosswise.

½ lb. of Swiss cheese; or, as the Swiss prefer, ¼ lb. each of two varieties of it.

1 small (8¼ ounce) can of tiny carrots.

1 long, thin loaf of crusty French bread.

Preparations

Start the oven to bring it to 400°. Put the oxtail pieces in a saucepan with a removable handle, and with the handle removed, put it in the oven for twenty minutes. Meanwhile, peel and slice into ½-inch pieces 2 medium onions and 2 carrots, and put the slices on a plate with ¼ teaspoon of thyme, ¼ teaspoon of marjoram, 5 stalks of parsley, a bay leaf, 2 cloves, a clove of garlic crushed, ten grinds on the pepper grinder, and 1 teaspoonful of salt.

After twenty minutes restore the handle to the pan, and remove it from the oven: the oxtail pieces will be dark brown from their baking and will have made from their juice a glaze on the pan's bottom. Add 2 quarts of water and with a wooden spoon deglaze the pan over brisk heat on the top of the stove. Reduce the heat, and allow the broth to come to a boil slowly; as it approaches a boil, a heavy foam will appear; remove it with the skimmer, and reskim as new foam appears. After twenty minutes' simmering the soup will be relatively clear. Turn into it then the vegetables, herbs, and other seasonings from the plate and allow it to simmer for two hours. As it boils away, add water to keep its volume constant. After two hours' simmering, strain off the soup from the meat and seasonings into a bowl in which you can refrigerate it; pick out the oxtail pieces from the seasonings, and wash them under running water to remove any herb fragments, and return them to the soup. Refrigerate until you wish to use it.

Cut the Swiss cheese into ¼-inch cubes, and refrigerate in a moistened dish towel.

Cooking

15 minutes

Remove the fat that will have solidified on the top of the refrigerated soup with a spoon or the skimmer. Set the soup to warm on moderate heat. Set a tablespoonful of arrowroot flour to soften in ½ cup of marsala or sherry.

10 minutes

Rub a fry pan with a crushed clove of garlic and pour into the garlicky pan ¼ cup of white wine seasoned with five grates of nutmeg on the nutmeg grater (⅛ teaspoonful); set to soften a teaspoonful of flour in some white liqueur, traditionally, white Swiss cherry brandy, kirsch; vodka will do.

5 minutes

Drain the liquid from the can of tiny carrots, and add them to the simmering soup. Thicken it with the arrowroot flour softened in the half cup of wine, without allowing it to boil again. If you like French bread warm, start the oven and leave the bread in it till you are ready to serve the soup.

Serve the clear, wine-rich, thickened soup in soup plates with a fork and a soupspoon so that you can eat the now-tender meat of the oxtail and the soup with the two implements. Serve some of the French bread with it, leaving the rest in the unlit oven for the fondue.

When you are ready for the fondue, excuse yourself briefly to make it. Add the ¼-inch cheese cubes to the seasoned wine, and warm the mixture over moderate heat on the top of the stove, stirring it, then beating it as the cheese melts, with a perforated spoon or beating whip, until the melting cheese makes it a consistent paste. Add the flour softened in the liqueur to smooth out the paste. For classic service, the fondue should be poured into a cocotte and served over a table warmer with the rest of the French bread: each guest breaks off a piece of the bread, spears it on a fork (the Swiss use special two-tined forks with an insulating handle), and stirs it in the bubbling fondue on the warmer. As the fondue goes on bubbling, it gradually forms a brown crust on the cocotte's bottom which is regarded as its culmination. Eating a fondue can enjoyably occupy a good twenty minutes!

Conversation piece: Oxtail soup from its invention has been one of the great and nourishing soups, relatively clear, thick enough to stick to the lips. "One of our eminent colleagues, M. Suzanne, in a very interesting study of English cookery, has explained the origin of this dish. 'At the time of the revocation of the Edict of Nantes, a large number of Huguenots took refuge in London, where they formed a kind of French colony in a quarter of the city occupied by tanners. Buying from the butchers the skins of beef animals, the tanners made no use of the tails, and gave them to the poor exiles of the quarter, who utilized them in a kind of soup. One day a rich and philanthropic gourmet, visiting the Huguenots, was initiated into the mysteries of this excellent soup, and introduced it into high society, where it became fashionable as tanners' soup.' "—*L'Art Culinaire Français*, pp. 940–41.

Fondue is eaten with a light white wine or with a *vin rosé;* either can be begun with the soup.

Menu 19

Pâté de foie gras ***Asparagus Hollandaise***

Luncheon for two

A SOPHISTICATED luncheon, particularly appropriate when fresh asparagus is at its best.

Shopping list

Pâté de foie gras, preferably in loaf form, from which slices are cut, thinly coated with goose fat, and with truffles in the *pâté,* such as can be found in specialty shops open or in cans; an alternative is the fine *pâté* that comes in a small porcelain pot, served in its pot and spooned out.

2½ lbs. of fresh asparagus, i.e., a bunch; to be preferred for this meal are the largest stalks that can be found; an alternative is the fine white canned Belgian asparagus; distinctly in third place but possible are frozen asparagus spears.

6 French rolls.

Preparations

Trim the asparagus stalks to the length your steamer will accommodate. Scrub the tips gently with a vegetable brush under cold running water. Lay each stalk on the kitchen bench and pare the tough outer skin with your slitted vegetable knife, beginning each paring about halfway down the stock, and taking rather more off the bottom ends. With asparagus thus pared, you can enjoy the fine inner meat of the stem's bottom. Arrange the stalks parallel in the steamer ready for later cooking.

Extract the juice of one lemon and add to it enough white vinegar, preferably white wine vinegar, to yield ¼ cup, and then an equal amount of water to yield a total of ½ cup. In the top of a double boiler directly over the heat bring this ½ cup of liquid, seasoned by ten grinds on the pepper grinder, to a boil, and leave it boiling till it has reduced to not more than 2 tablespoonfuls. If by inadvertence it reduces to a glaze, so long as it is not burned, you can bring it back by the addition of 2 tablespoonfuls of water and brief boiling. Separate 2 egg yolks from their whites and put them in a small bowl; set the bowl in the refrigerator, as egg yolks are quickly contaminated in the open air. You have now completed the preparations for the actual making of Hollandaise sauce.

Cooking ***15 minutes***

Start toward a boil a pan of water into which your steamer fits.

10 minutes

Put the steamer on the now-boiling water. Start toward a boil the double boiler, with the top in it with its basic flavoring for Hollandaise sauce. Beat the separated yolks of two eggs with an egg beater till they turn a lighter yellow.

5 minutes

If in this reheating the liquid in the double boiler top has too much reduced, again bring its volume back to 2 tablespoonfuls by the addition of water. Move the double boiler with boiling water in its bottom to the kitchen shelf; give the egg yolks an additional beat, and pour into them the basic seasoning from the double boiler top; beat briefly again and pour the seasoned mixture back into the double boiler top over the hot water in its bottom. Stir steadily with a wooden spoon, as the seasoned egg yolks thicken, and to smooth them, add 1 tablespoonful of hot water from the double boiler bottom. Stirring steadily, add cold butter from the refrigerator 1 cubic inch at a time, to a total of from 2 to 3 cubic inches: you have added enough when the hot sauce is the consistency of cold mayonnaise. Finally add and stir in 1 teaspoonful of salt. In my experience, you can safely leave this Hollandaise over the still-hot but cooling water of the double boiler's bottom without its curdling if you give it an occasional stir. If it should curdle, and it has not with me for many years, you can bring it back by quickly separating and adding another beaten egg yolk; in my experience, Hollandaise does not curdle over diminishing heat; by the same token, it is difficult to warm up without curdling.

As you sit down to enjoy the *pâté*, turn off the heat under the steamer of asparagus, to allow it to finish cooking and keep warm: this timing should produce asparagus that is still bright green, cooked through, and tender enough to enjoy, in part because of the paring. Most Americans overcook asparagus!

Serve the asparagus on a platter with the stalks heaped parallel; the Hollandaise should be served in an only slightly warmed bowl; a hot bowl can curdle it. French rolls should accompany both the *pâté* and the asparagus; they require no butter on the table, since the *pâté* first and the Hollandaise later more than make up for it.

The *pâté* deserves a red wine, and a red wine goes equally well with the asparagus, unless you wish to shift to a white: this is a meal in which a half bottle of each would do well.

As a dessert for this sophisticated luncheon I should have prepared in advance Crêpes Suzette, as I do with minimum effort by following the procedure described below (p. 192). By following it, all you have to do to produce them on time is to remove them from the slow oven and flame them.

Menu 20

Stuffed Pancakes *Artichokes Vinaigrette*

Luncheon for two

ANOTHER sophisticated luncheon which has the advantage of being prepared entirely in advance.

Shopping list

½ pint of cottage cheese, or, better, if you can get to an Italian shop, ½ lb. of ricotta.

2 large artichokes.

Preparations

Start to boil a kettle three quarters full of water salted with 1 tablespoonful of salt. With your sharp chef's knife, cut off the stem of the artichokes at the point where their leaves begin; similarly, cut off the thorny tops of the leaves with a single crosswise cut ½ inch down the leaves. When the water in the kettle comes to a boil, boil them until the tine of a fork easily penetrates their bottoms, as it usually will after fifteen minutes' boiling. It would be pleasant if cooked artichokes could retain their green, but I know of no way of cooking them to requisite tenderness and of retaining it; inevitably, to be edible, they must be a darkened green. When they are cooked, set them tops down to drain, and then, if time presses, refrigerate them to cool them in time. If you want to spare your guest the trouble, and want to serve them with real elegance, remove the inner leaves and the "choke" when they have cooled: this can be done with the bowl of a teaspoon, used not to cut, but to pull; even the feathery "choke" will come out with gentle pulling. If you are successful in this, as you can be with almost no practice, the outer leaves will remain intact, with a cylindrical opening inside them down to the edible bottom.

Make six or more French pancakes from two thirds of the basic recipe as given below (p. 192). Prepare the stuffing for them as follows: beat one egg in a medium-sized bowl, stir into it the cottage cheese or ricotta seasoned with 1 teaspoonful of salt and ten grates of nutmeg on the nutmeg grater (¼ teaspoonful). Divide this stuffing equally on the center of each pancake and fold them over it into square packages: sides in first, then the two ends. Butter a baking pan in which the pancakes can be served, and arrange them, folded side down, in it. Sprinkle them with spaghetti cheese and place on each 1 tablespoonful of sour cream.

Make sauce vinaigrette, i.e., a salad dressing with chopped onions and herbs (see below, p. 174).

Cooking

Start the oven to bring it to 350°. ***20 minutes***

15 minutes

Put the stuffed pancakes in the buttered pan in the 350° oven.

Serve the stuffed pancakes in their baking dish. They are a luncheon in themselves. If you feel the need of something with them, try some good American pickles, preferably of the "bread-and-butter" variety.

Serve the artichokes as a second course, with the sauce vinaigrette in a bowl apart.

This meal needs no preliminary. An unusual and appropriate dessert would be the Danish dish, *rød grød*, German, *Rote Grütze* (see p. 189), which can also, indeed must be, prepared in advance.

For this meal a white wine is called for.

Conversation piece: How to eat an artichoke is always a minor subject for convivial debate. The bottom is supposed to be the climax, so that most amateurs of this vegetable save it for the last, eating first the delicate meat at each leaf's bottom by pulling it through their teeth. My preference is for gently breaking off all the leaves from the bottom in a regular circle round it, eating the bottom first (with knife and fork) and finishing or tapering off with the leaves. (The root of this preference is that if I have eaten the leaf bottoms first I tend to have had enough artichoke by the time I come to the bottom itself: if I eat it first, I can have as much more as I happen to want from the leaves).

Menu 21

Coquilles St. Jacques Avocado Salad

Luncheon for two

ANOTHER choice luncheon which can also be prepared in advance.

Shopping list

½ lb. scallops, preferably the small "bay" scallops, though in this recipe the large "sea" scallops will serve; if you use them, cut them in quarters.

¼ lb. cooked shrimps.

¼ lb. mushrooms, preferably small.

1 avocado pear. If you are buying it on the day of your luncheon, ask your fruit man to pick you out one that is ready to eat: it should be slightly soft to the touch, and it may be that the central stone will rattle when you shake it; knowing when an avocado is really ready is an art. I try to practice it by buying mine some days before I want to use them, leaving them in a warm, sunlit place, e.g., on a window sill, and picking out the one which seems to me readiest.

Salad greens, for example, a bunch of water cress, or a head of curly chicory.

Preparations

Shell the shrimps with your fingers and remove the back strip, together with the black intestinal strip that lies under it; or, better, do both operations at once with the shrimp deveiner included in desirable kitchen equipment.

Remove the mushroom stems (saving them for other uses) and wash and slice the heads in ⅛-inch slices; leave them drying on a paper towel.

Melt 1 cubic inch of butter in a double boiler and stir into it 2 tablespoonfuls of flour to make a white roux; let it cook over the hot water for at least fifteen minutes.

Put in a saucepan ½ cup of white wine, 3 tablespoonfuls of chopped shallots or onions, 5 stalks of parsley, ⅛ teaspoonful each of thyme and marjoram, ½ teaspoonful of salt, and five grinds on the pepper grinder. Add to this mixture the scallops, bring it to a boil, and let it simmer for ten minutes. Through a fine sieve strain this liquid on the now cooked white roux in the double boiler, and continuing to cook it over hot water, stir it as it thickens into a smooth, velvety sauce. Add to it the strained-off scallops (picking them out from the fragments of the seasonings), the cleaned shrimps, and the sliced mushroom heads. When all these ingredients have amalgamated into a thickened mixture, divide the solid components (scallops, shrimps, and mushroom slices) among 4 scallop shells, lifting them out of the sauce with a perforated spoon. Then arrange the shells in a baking pan: you can set each shell in a corner so that it is level and does not rock. When the shells are thus stabilized, divide the remaining sauce among them. Finish the *Coquilles St. Jacques* by sprinkling bread crumbs over each and by dotting each with butter, 1 cubic inch among the four. They are now ready for their final brief cooking. If you have prepared them well in advance, refrigerate before using.

Wash and dry whatever salad greens you procured. Cut the avocado in two, lengthwise around its stone; remove the stone and the skin; if it is an amenable fruit, and is really ripe, its tough skin will peel off in your fingers; if refractory, though still ripe, you may have to peel it, like other fruit, with a knife. When you have achieved two neatly peeled halves, lay them on a platter, flat side down, and immediately sprinkle them with lemon juice so that they do not turn brown. On the platter slice them through crosswise in ½-inch slices. Arrange around them choice pieces of whatever green salad you procured, and refrigerate.

Make a basic salad dressing (see p. 172) with less vinegar than usual, to take into account the acidity of the lemon juice you have already sprinkled on the avocado.

Cooking

Start the oven to bring it to 350°. ***15 minutes***

10 minutes

Put the *Coquilles St. Jacques* in their baking pan in the 350° oven.

5 minutes

Look at the *Coquilles St. Jacques*: if they are not beginning to brown a bit on the top, start the broiler, and give them a brief exposure to its flame to brown their tops just before serving.

To serve, lift the shells from the baking pan with the skimmer and arrange them on a platter. If you like food really hot, you can eat their contents directly from the shells; or if you prefer food cooler, it is in order to transfer their contents to your plate.

Serve the sliced avocado with the garnish of salad greens as it comes from the refrigerator with the dressing in a bowl.

Traditionally, *Coquilles St. Jacques* begin a meal, so that this one calls for no preliminary. For dessert try a *riz au lait*, a European rice pudding, and to my taste superior to what goes by the name in the United States (see below, p. 188). It, too, should be prepared in advance.

This is a meal for a white wine throughout.

Menu 22

Lobster (or Shrimp) Newburg Artichokes

Luncheon, dinner, or supper for two

A FAMOUS dish, but easy to prepare in its classic form.

Shopping list

½ lb. of lobster meat from a reliable fish seller, but not the canned variety, as it will disintegrate in this use of it; or, if you prefer, and are accustomed to handling lobsters, enough live lobsters to yield, when boiled and open, the same amount of meat, i.e., about 2 pounds of live lobsters. Alternatively ½ lb. of shrimps, again for the same reason, not canned; raw or boiled, as you prefer.

2 large artichokes.

½ pint of cream, (this time, sweet) light or heavy.

1 small loaf of fine white bread, thinly sliced.

Preparations

Boil and open the lobsters, if you bought them alive (or boil and shell the shrimp). The lobster meat, from the claws, arms, and body, should be cut into inch-long pieces (the shrimps are used whole). Refrigerate till used.

With your sharp chef's knife cut off the stem of the artichokes at the point where the leaves begin; similarly cut off the thorny tops of the leaves with a single crosswise cut ½ inch down the leaves. Leave them soaking in cold water till used.

Cooking

30 minutes

Start toward a boil a kettle three quarters full of water salted with 1 tablespoonful of salt. Separate the yolks of 3 eggs and beat them in a small bowl till they turn a lighter yellow; dilute with 1 tablespoonful of cream, and briefly beat again.

25 minutes

In the top of a double boiler directly on the heat fry the lobster (or shrimp) in 1 cubic inch of butter until the meat turns golden and a glaze begins to form on the bottom of the pan; during this frying, season with 1 teaspoonful of salt and a dash of cayenne pepper.

20 minutes

When the meat is golden, add ½ cup of marsala (or sherry) and let the wine reduce over moderate heat to about half its volume.

15 minutes

Add the remainder of the cream and leave the lobster simmering in it over low heat: there is no harm in its boiling gently at this point. Start the artichokes cooking in the boiling water in the kettle.

10 minutes

Make six pieces of white toast; trim off the crusts and cut them across once diagonally to make small triangles; put the triangles in a warm place (e.g., the oven at lowest possible heat) to dry and crisp.

5 minutes

Put the double boiler top in which the lobster has been simmering in the cream into the double boiler bottom filled with warm water from the tap over moderate heat; re-beat briefly and add to the sauce the 3 beaten egg yolks, stirring them in well, and continuing to stir till the initial foam has disappeared and the sauce thickens. Meanwhile, remove the artichokes from the water; reduce the heat under it to a simmer; put the artichokes in a sieve, bottom up, to drain, and set the sieve across the kettle's edges so that they are kept warm and continue to cook a bit.

If the newburg sauce is thickened by this time, and *if* you turn off the heat under the double boiler bottom, it will remain consistent i.e., not curdle, while you take time out for a final cocktail. This is, admittedly, a meal that requires last-minute cooking; but at this point it is under control, and the cook deserves a few minutes of relaxation.

To serve, give the newburg a final tablespoonful of marsala (or sherry), stir it in, and pour the newburg into a "vegetable dish." Arrange the triangles of toast round its edge, with the apex of each triangle in the sauce, to make a border, with the triangles' bases an even line around the dish. Serve the newburg at the table on each plate, and garnish it there with the triangles of toast.

To serve the artichokes, put 2 cubic inches of butter in a place warm enough to melt it as you serve the newburg. As you change the plates after enjoying it, put the melted butter on the heat briefly and serve it with the artichokes in a bowl. This is a meal with a vegetable (*légume*) instead of a salad; and this is a *légume* which can be made more like the expected salad by serving it with wedges of lemon to provide the acid of the salad.

This meal admits no preliminary: the newburg is so much like a soup that any soup is inadmissible; its flavor is so delicate that the idea of a hors d'oeuvre is hardly allowable. If you want to extend it I suggest what for me is a fine and neglected dessert: crystallized ginger–moist, sugary, hot, and, somehow, digestive.

It also goes well with the end of the chilled white wine this meal deserves.

Menu 23

Lobster (or Shrimp) Américaine Pilaf

Dinner for two

ANOTHER famous dish, also, with slight adaptations, easy to prepare in its classic form.

Shopping list

½ lb. of lobster meat (or ½ lb. of shrimp) with the alternatives of Menu 22.

2 tomatoes.

Salad, as you will.

Preparations

Prepare the lobster (or shrimp) as in Menu 22, lobster meat in inch-long pieces; shrimp whole.

Wash and chop enough parsley to yield 2 tablespoonfuls. Peel and chop finely 3 shallots (or grate half an onion).

Bring a saucepan of water to a boil and immerse each tomato in the boiling water for a slow count of ten (seconds); when the tomatoes have cooled, you will find that the skin comes off easily with a knife. When you have peeled the tomatoes, cut them into quarters, and under cold running water, with your fingers, wash out the seeds; the more you mangle them in the process the better; put them aside on a plate for later use.

Wash and dry the salad; make the salad dressing.

Cooking

Start the oven to bring it to 350°. *35 minutes*

30 minutes

To make what is an unadorned pilaf, melt 1 cubic inch of butter in a saucepan, and stir into it ½ cup of rice; add ½ teaspoonful of salt and five grinds on the pepper grinder. Stir over moderate heat till the grains of rice are thoroughly coated with butter and turn transparent. Add 1 cup of water; bring the mixture to a boil, pour it into a cocotte, and set it to cook in the 350° oven.

25 minutes

In a saucepan, over medium heat, fry the chopped shallots (or onion) together with 1 crushed clove of garlic, not allowing them to brown; add the lobster pieces (or shrimp) and continue frying till they are golden and a glaze begins to form on the bottom of the pan; add ½ teaspoonful of salt and a dash of cayenne pepper as the frying proceeds.

25 minutes

When the pieces are golden, pour over the meat ¼ cup of brandy (whisky will do, but sweetens the dish slightly); as it steams up, light it with a match, standing back, because it may flare up momentarily; keep it flaming as long as you can by shaking the pan. As the flame dies, add ½ a small can of tomato paste, the mangled tomatoes, ½ cup of white wine, ½ (5 ounces) can of beef consommé, and 1 tablespoonful of chopped parsley. Stir the mixture together, cover, and leave simmering over low heat.

20 minutes

Check the progress of the pilaf in the oven; by this time it will have partly thickened; stir it with a two-tined fork.

10 minutes

With a perforated spoon remove the lobster pieces (or shrimp) from the sauce and put them on the platter on which you wish to serve them; keep them warm. Remove the crushed clove of garlic and put the sauce through the Foley Food Mill, returning the purée to the saucepan to reduce into a thick sauce over low heat. There is no need for concern if some of the unpuréed sauce clings to the pieces.

To serve, finish the thickened sauce by melting into it 1 cubic inch of butter; pour a third of it over the lobster pieces (or shrimp) on the platter, and sprinkle over the remaining tablespoonful of chopped parsley; serve the rest of the sauce in a bowl apart. Serve the pilaf in its cocotte.

This is, as noted, a slight adaptation of the classic recipe for *Homard Américaine:* in the classic recipe, it is made with pieces of a live lobster still in their shells, and so is richer from the shells and all the fat and meat that clings to them; but most American cooks feel some prejudice about cutting up a live lobster. (As a hardened hand with lobsters, I have done it; the product is richer, but it is something of a chore at the table to get the cooked meat out of the shells). It should be noted, since this recipe is relatively unfamiliar on this side of the Atlantic, that the Sauce Américaine of its title was probably originally Sauce Amoricaine, i.e., Breton, from the old term for Brittany, Amorica. If any of this Sauce Américaine remains unused in the serving bowl, guard it well (i.e., refrigerate it covered) for other uses: it is a sauce in itself, and is delicious, for example, with poached eggs on toast.

Again this meal somehow admits no preliminary. An appropriate dessert would be *babas au rhum:* you can usually buy babas, a kind of coarse individual raised bread cake, in good French bakeries, already moistened with a rummy syrup; add a little more pure rum before serving them.

This is a meal for a rather stout white wine.

Menu 24

Deviled Crab   Salade Belle Hortense
Pâté de foie gras in aspic

Luncheon for two

AN EASY luncheon, for all its elegance, because mainly prepared in advance.

Shopping list

In the case of this luncheon, your shopping should be done the afternoon of the day before.

½ lb. of crab meat, best in the form of one of the huge claws of Alaska king crab which now are on the market in fine condition, frozen; alternatively any frozen crab meat, but not canned meat, which usually seems to have been so much cooked in canning that it goes to shreds in further cooking.

1 bunch of celery, preferably celery hearts that are almost entirely usable.

1 can of inexpensive *pâté de foie gras.*
1 can of sliced beets.
1 pound of walnuts.
1 small jar of sweet gherkins.
1 small bottle of capers (if you like them).

Preparations

This is a meal that calls for preparations the previous day, e.g., during the evening, and correspondingly calls for a relatively brief period of cooking on the day it is served.

The previous day make the aspics of *pâté de foie gras* in individual molds. Because this apparently difficult procedure is actually both easy and quick, it is given here with its timing.

30 minutes

Put to soften in ¼ cup of white wine 1 teaspoonful of unflavored gelatin: this has proved to be the precise amount when used as below with "consommé with gelatin added," such as produces a jellied consommé when refrigerated; more produces an aspic that is tough. Put 6 individual aspic molds in a baking tin (simply for convenience and to steady them) in the refrigerator to chill.

25 minutes

Add the now pasty gelatin and wine to a 10½-ounce can of beef "consommé with gelatin added" in the upper part of a double boiler directly over medium heat, and cook (not boil) until the gelatin has fully dissolved. While it is dissolving, break out a tray of ice cubes and put them in the lower part of the double boiler to "cook with cold!"

20 minutes

Remove the aspic from the heat and set the double boiler top on the ice in its bottom; for quick results you should use enough ice so that the pan's bottom is directly on it. Stir occasionally as it cools. While it is cooling, open the can of *pâté de foie gras:* if you can, empty it, keeping the *pâté* in a single piece, on a piece of aluminum foil on the kitchen shelf and cut it into cubes small enough to fit in the individual molds without their corners' obtruding to its sides; an alternative procedure is to shape the *pâté* into cubes with the flat blade of a table knife, remembering in the process that clean fingers are sometimes the most useful kitchen implement.

15 minutes

Give the aspic its final flavoring, ¼ cup of marsala (or sherry), and pour enough of it into the chilled molds from the refrigerator to fill each mold half full; return them to the refrigerator. With a clean butter brush gently brush a little aspic over the cubes of *pâté* on the foil, simply in order that the aspic will cling better to their greasy sides. If the aspic in the double boiler top is thickening, remove it from the ice; keep it cool and liquid from this point on, and you may be surprised at how quickly it will solidify when once cold.

5 minutes

By now the aspic in the molds in the refrigerator should be quite firm. Removing them from the refrigerator, put on the center of the hardened aspic in each a cube of *pâté:* you can most handily lift them from the foil with the blunt tip of a table knife, and then steer them into place with it and your fingers. Fill each mold with the remaining liquid aspic; if it should have hardened too much to pour, bring it back to liquidity by letting it reheat very slightly over hot water; as you will learn, it can easily be manipulated back and forth in this way. Return the molds in their baking pan to the refrigerator, to solidify there thoroughly overnight. Pour any leftover aspic into some small receptacle and refrigerate it also.

The previous day prepare also the Salade Belle Hortense, one of the classic *salades composées*. Make first sauce rémoulade (see below, p. 157). Shell the walnuts, keeping as many of the halves as possible in one piece; chop the inevitably broken halves into small bits with your chef's knife. Cut crosswise into ⅛-inch slices the better inner stalks of the celery, and mix into the celery and the chopped nuts half of the sauce rémoulade; refrigerate this mixture and the remainder of the sauce.

The morning of your luncheon, finish both the aspics and the salad. Have ready the platter on which you wish to serve the aspics. Fill a pan with water as hot as it comes from the faucet and, holding the rim of each mold with your fingers, dip briefly into it each mold of now firmly solidified aspic only as long as is necessary to free the aspic from the mold, a matter of perhaps ten seconds; planning generally how you want them on the platter (two rows of three, or two rows of two, with one each at the platter's end, if its ends are rounded), turn them on to the platter in this general arrangement; you can regularize it when all of them are turned out by moving them with a spatula slipped under them. Don't be alarmed that, in releasing them from the molds in the hot water, some of the exterior aspic may have melted and thus will run on the platter. When the individual aspics are arranged as you want them on the platter, with a spoon stir up and chop the leftover aspic which has also been solidifying in its dish in the refrigerator into a sparkling stiff paste, and spread it on the platter between or around the individual aspics; it will thus cover any aspic that ran as you turned the molds out. Or, if you had no aspic left over to serve this purpose, you can tidy up the platter just before serving by scraping this runoff into a similar sparkling paste just before you serve. Refrigerate the platter as thus arranged, and keep it refrigerated till just before serving.

To finish the Salade Belle Hortense add to the refrigerated mixture the half of the sauce rémoulade which you kept for this purpose; much of the other half will by now have been absorbed by the celery, as was intended. Open the can of sliced beets, drain the slices, and dry them between two paper towels. Transfer the celery in its sauce rémoulade to a serving bowl, and with a spoon level its top surface. Arrange the beet slices, thoroughly dry so that none of their red juice will run into the salad, in a circle around the bowl's sides. Arrange the unbroken halves of the walnuts in interior circles, mounding up any surplus in the center. Wash and chop enough parsley to yield 1 tablespoonful, and sprinkle it evenly over the top, with a nice blending of its bright green, the dark red of the beets, and the brown of the nuts. Refrigerate till just before serving.

On the morning of your luncheon you would do well, too, in the interests of minimizing the final "cooking time," to have the crab ready to cook: if, as preferably, it is in the form of a frozen claw of Alaska king crab, cut the claw crosswise with your sturdiest knife used as a cleaver enough times to enable you to extract the meat in pieces an inch long; if, as often happens, it comes out in longer pieces, cut them to inch lengths. Refrigerate the pieces. Chop finely 3 peeled shallots (or half an onion).

With these preparations, the actual "cooking time" for this luncheon will be hardly more than twenty minutes.

Cooking

·Peel and chop 3 shallots (or half onion). ***25 minutes***

20 minutes

Fry the chopped shallots (or onion) in 1 cubic inch of butter, not letting them brown.

15 minutes

Fry the crab meat in the shallots and butter till golden and a glaze is forming on the bottom of the pan; add ½ teaspoonful of salt and a dash of cayenne pepper.

10 minutes

Deglaze by flaming in brandy (or whisky): pour over the crab ⅛ cup of brandy (or whisky), and as it steams, light the vapor with a match; keep it flaming as long as it will by shaking the pan. When the flame dies out, add a cup of cream (½ pint) into which you have dissolved 1 tablespoonful of prepared mustard. Leave the mixture on moderate heat, simmering.

5 minutes

Start the broiler. With a perforated spoon tranfer the crab meat to 3 scallop shells stabilized in a baking dish; divide the remaining sauce among them; sprinkle them with bread crumbs; dot with 1 cubic inch of butter divided among them; finish them under the broiler by exposure to its flame till the butter has melted, the bread crumbs have browned, and the deviled crab is sizzling.

Serve on a platter, first one to a person, and divide the second.

Follow the deviled crab with the Salade Belle Hortense and the individual aspics from the refrigerator.

This meal admits no preliminary. An admirable dessert would be flamed pears (see p. 186).

A white wine is called for throughout.

Menu 25

Filet of Sole Marguéry   *Steamed Potatoes*

Dinner for two

THE PRIDE of the finest restaurants, sole Marguéry, though a last-minute dish, is by no means beyond the reach of the amateur cook.

Shopping list

2 filets of lemon sole; if you cannot get lemon sole, gray sole is the next best, and failing that, enough of the smaller filets of flounder for two.

¼ lb. of boiled shrimp.

6 shelled-out oysters.

1 lb. of small new potatoes.

1 bunch of fresh dill if you can find it; if not, parsley will do.

Salad, as you will.

Preparations

Wash the filets of sole in running cold water and dry them on paper towels. Cut each filet twice along its center strip to eliminate the strip: often it contains tiny bone ends (you can feel them with your fingers), but in this instance you will utilize this strip, so keep it. Cut off the thin ends of the resulting pieces and any ragged edges. Use these trimmings to make a fish stock (*fumet de poisson*). Put them with 2 cups of water and 1 cup of white wine in a saucepan, together with one small grated onion, 5 stalks of parsley, ten grinds on the pepper grinder, ¼ teaspoonful of thyme, and ¼ teaspoonful of marjoram. Simmer for thirty minutes. As you start it, melt 1 cubic inch of butter and 2 tablespoonfuls of flour in the top of a double boiler over hot water, and allow them to cook together for the balance of thirty minutes, to make a white *roux*.

Shell the shrimp. Peel the potatoes into regular shapes, and leave them in cold water to prevent their turning brown. Chop enough dill (or parsley) to yield 1 tablespoonful. Wash and dry the salad; prepare the salad dressing.

After thirty minutes strain off the fish broth from its seasonings. Stir 2 cups into the white *roux* in the double boiler top, retaining the rest for later use, and continue to cook in the double boiler until it becomes a clear, velvety sauce known in French as "Fish velvet," *velouté de poisson.* If, as is possible, you have been carrying through these preparations well in advance, refrigerate the fish, the fish velvet, and the remainder of the fish stock till you wish to start the actual cooking.

Cooking

25 minutes

Start the oven to bring it to 350°. Start toward a boil a panful of water over which your steamer will fit. Butter a baking dish that will stand a direct broiler flame, and arrange in it the pieces of sole; sprinkle over them the remainder of the fish stock, adding to it, if necessary, enough water to make it total ½ cup (the original 3 cups will have reduced somewhat).

20 minutes

Put the fish in the stock into the 350° oven and the potatoes into the covered steamer over the now-boiling water. Warm the fish velvet in the double boiler, adding to it the shelled shrimp and the oysters and their juice.

15 minutes

Light the broiler. Separate 2 egg yolks from their whites, and beat in a small bowl until they turn a lighter yellow; dilute with 1 tablespoonful of milk and briefly beat again.

10 minutes

Pour the beaten egg yolks into the fish velvet in the double boiler, reducing the heat under it so that it is kept well below a boil, and stir as the egg yolks thicken the velvet into a creamy sauce. Stir in 1 cubic inch of butter and 1 teaspoonful of salt.

5 minutes

Remove the poaching fish from the oven and, holding the pieces with a spatula, pour off any of the remaining fish stock. Rearrange the pieces in the middle of the dish, allowing it to cool somewhat: you are dealing with a sauce that can curdle (*sauce vin blanc,* from the wine that went into the stock), and from here on you must minimize its heating.

To serve, pour the sauce into the somewhat cooled dish, distributing around its sides the shrimp and oysters. Melt 1 cubic inch of butter; put the potatoes in a vegetable dish and sprinkle over them first the chopped dill (or parsley) and pour over them the melted butter; keep warm. At the very last minute expose the fish in its sauce to the by now very hot broiler, with the broiler door open, never taking your eyes from it, until just as brown spots begin to appear on the surface of the sauce, as they will in a matter of seconds. Serve at once.

The necessity of preparing this dish at the very last moment precludes any preliminary. As a dessert that can have been prepared in advance and that suits the elegance of the meal, try apricots Condé (see p. 189).

This is a meal for a white wine, and it can be a richer one, such as one of the white burgundies.

Menu 26

Veal Chasseur String Beans

Dinner for two

A CLASSIC way of cooking veal, this time in a brown sauce.

Shopping list

½ lb. of veal scaloppini, as in Menu 4.

1 package of "French-cut" frozen string beans, generally preferable unless you can buy fresh string beans that are the delicacy that is their European counterpart: European beans are tiny—hardly more than ⅛ inch broad, and tasty—grown for taste, rather than size; a few times a year you obtain their nearest American equivalent by watching for fresh string beans which, while in general grown for size, include a fair proportion that are small if not tiny; when I see such beans, I buy 2 pounds or more, sort them into large and small, have a good meal of the small ones cooked as here, and cut the rest, cook them, and have them cold as string-bean salad. Of course if

you have your own garden, you can pick your string beans when they are still tiny.

½ lb. of fresh mushrooms.

Salad, as you will.

Preparations

Remove the stems from the mushrooms; wash and slice the heads in ⅛-inch slices crosswise. Chop finely 3 shallots (or half an onion). Chop enough parsley to yield 1 tablespoonful.

Make clear brown sauce (see p. 152); add during its cooking 1 tablespoonful of tomato paste or ketchup.

Wash and dry the salad; make the salad dressing.

Cooking

Start the oven to bring it to 300°. ***30 minutes***

25 minutes

Fry the pieces of veal in 1 cubic inch of butter, precisely as in Menu 4. Fry the first pieces till they are merely white and set them aside in a baking dish; as their juice has mixed with the butter, a brown glaze will have begun to form on the frying pan's bottom which will augment as you fry the other pieces; you can give them a fine brown without overcooking them by rubbing them gently in this glaze as they fry; as they attain it, set them aside in the baking dish and return the first white pieces briefly to the pan for their final coloration. Put the pieces in the 300° oven to cook through.

20 minutes

Fry the chopped shallots in the frying pan, adding ½ cubic inch of butter if it is needed, over moderate heat, being careful not to let the glaze on the pan's bottom burn; add the mushroom slices, scattering over them 1 teaspoonful of salt and ten grinds on the pepper grinder; as the mushrooms yield their juice under the influence of the salt, you can begin to deglaze the pan with your wooden spoon. Finish the deglazing by adding ½ cup of white wine and leave the mixture simmering.

15 minutes

Start to boil a saucepan of water seasoned with 2 teaspoonfuls of salt and ten grinds on the pepper grinder. Pour the clear brown sauce you prepared into the fry pan, and continue to simmer.

10 minutes

Put the string beans into the now boiling water for ten minutes' cooking.

5 minutes

Remove the veal from the oven and turn off the heat; set in the oven with the door open the platter on which you wish to serve the veal. Put the veal slices briefly in the sauce in the frying pan and pour into it the juice that will have accumulated in the baking pan. Arrange them on the warmed serving platter and pour over them about a third of the sauce, putting the remaining two thirds into a bowl to serve apart. Sprinkle the chopped parsley over the veal on the platter.

To serve the beans, drain off the water in which they have cooked and return them in the same saucepan to moderate heat; let them steam briefly over it to eliminate the last vestiges of the water, and stir into them with the two-tined fork (to avoid mashing them) 1 cubic inch of butter. The ten-minute boiling, together with this final cooking, should yield beans that are sufficiently cooked and still bright green.

Since both the veal and the beans can be kept warm without serious deterioration, this is a meal in which you can enjoy a preliminary course, such as a fine cream of pea soup.

For dessert a bowl of dried figs, dates, and assorted nuts would go well.

This meal calls for a light red wine.

Menu 27

Roast Duck Bigarade — Wild Rice

Dinner for two

ANOTHER classic, easy to prepare, with an American touch in the native wild rice.

Shopping list

1 duck, or two, the smallest you can buy. Have the butcher remove the neck; make sure that he gives you the liver.

½ lb. of wild rice.

2 oranges.

1 bunch of water cress.

Preparations

With the water cress still in its string, cut off in one cut the lower tougher parts of the stems; wash and set it to dry on paper towels.

Peel the oranges round and round so that the skin comes off in a strip, cutting deeply enough to remove a bit of the inner flesh, and so its outer membrane; over a plate, to catch the juice, cut lengthwise on each side of each membrane to obtain wedges of the clear flesh, knife in right hand, the orange in the left; squeeze the pulp to extract its final juice. Put aside separately the juice and the wedges for later use. Scrape off the flesh and some of the white inner skin from the strips you peeled from the oranges, and cut it crosswise in ⅛-inch slices; set them aside for later use.

Wash the duck inside and out and dry with paper towels. You would do well at this point (earlier if possible) to prepare the preliminary suggested for this meal, *foie gras,* the pure liver, not the *pâté;* put the duck liver in a small saucepan, sprinkle over it ¼ teaspoonful of salt, ten grinds on the pepper grinder, and ⅛ cup of brandy; add one whole clove, and let it sit as long as you can, up to several hours; if you are pressed for time, its cooking can begin at once, but it is better for this soaking. To cook, add ¼ cup of beef consommé and ¼ cup of marsala (or sherry), and simmer for half an hour, covered, over the lowest possible heat. Cool, and slice the liver in ¼-inch slices; serve on toast, glazing the slices on the toast with the thick juice which remains in the pan.

Cocking

60 minutes

Start the oven to bring it to 400°. Put the duck in the roasting pan; duck for roasting may be but need not be trussed, since the short legs of the American breed, unlike the French, stay down in place during roasting. For reasons noted below you should fold back the flap of skin at the neck and secure it to the back with a couple of stitches with your trussing needle and butcher's twine.

55 minutes

Put the duck in the 400° oven. This timing allows for fifty minutes' roasting; I prefer a bit less, not more than forty minutes; but most Americans like their duck, as their lamb, with all its pink cooked out. For roasting, duck neither requires nor wants any additional grease or moisture. All that is necessary during roasting is to be sure that the duck does not brown too rapidly; rather it should move gradually to the fine brown of the properly finished product. Be particularly careful, if in watching it you pull out the roasting pan, not to be burned by spattering fat; this spattering occurs if, in moving the pan, you tilt it down, so that the watery juices which have been accumulated inside the duck run out where the body has been opened at the rear; thus striking the fat which has been accumulating in the pan, they cause it to spatter, sometimes explosively. There is a simple way of avoiding this risk: put the duck in the oven with this rear opening at the back; the closed neck at the front will retain these juices till you want them.

30 minutes

Start a saucepan three fourths full of water seasoned with 1 tablespoonful of salt. Wash the wild rice in a colander under running cold water: it tends to be dusty.

25 minutes

Start the wild rice cooking in the now boiling water. Set 2 teaspoonfuls of arrowroot flour to soften in ½ cup of white wine. Make a special salad dressing for the water cress: ½ teaspoonful of salt dissolved in 3 tablespoonfuls of oil—no vinegar or pepper.

5 minutes

Remove the duck from the roasting pan, again being careful that none of its interior juices spill into the hot fat; pour off the fat, and then pour into the pan all the interior juice the duck will yield; keep the duck warm on the platter on which it is to be served in the oven with the door open. Put the pan on moderate heat on the top of the stove; let the interior juices boil briefly to add themselves to whatever glaze there is on the pan's bottom, and then deglaze with the orange juice you reserved for this purpose; add half of a 10½-ounce can of beef consommé, the white wine, and the arrowroot flour, and strain the resulting sauce through a fine sieve into a small saucepan, adding to it the thin slices of orange peel. Distribute the wedges of clear orange flesh around the duck on its platter. Pour over it a little of the sauce bigarade, and serve the rest in a bowl apart. The classic recipe calls for coloring this sauce with caramel, because, without it, it is unexpectedly light in color.

To serve the wild rice, drain it from its water in a colander while you are melting 1 cubic inch of butter in the pan in which it cooked; return it to the pan and stir it into the butter with a wooden spoon.

Both the duck and the wild rice can be kept warm without deterioration while you enjoy the suggested preliminary for this meal, the sliced duck liver on toast, a proper preview of the flavor of the main course.

Serve the buttered rice in a vegetable dish, and I would suggest serving at the same time the salad of water cress; for once, it is a salad that goes well with the main course, and the French often eat it, almost as a vegetable, with roast poultry.

Duck is never easy to carve. The prescribed method is, as with chicken, first to cut off the two legs; the hip joints at which you want to separate them from the body is always farther in than you expect! The breast meat is not taken off in slices, as with a chicken, but rather in long, triangular wedges, each with its share of the crusty skin.

You are likely to be having duck when chestnuts are in season and I suggest a Turinois as a dessert for this meal (see p. 191).

Duck calls for a rich red wine of the Burgundy type.

Menu 28

Braised Sweetbreads ***Asparagus Tips***

Dinner for two

THE FIRST of three final menus involving various forms of braising, sometimes said to be of the various forms of cooking the most costly and the most difficult to succeed with. It need be neither, as these menus will show.

Shopping list

In the case of this dinner your shopping should be done the afternoon of the day before.

A pair of veal sweetbreads. Ask the butcher to give you a solid piece of beef fat from the kidney region; explain that you want it for larding the sweetbreads, and that you want to do it yourself; if he offers to lard them for you, resist the suggestion for two reasons: first, he will almost surely lard them with salt pork, saying that it can't be done with beef fat; second, you don't want them larded in the first stage of their cooking.

A bunch of small asparagus stalks, or if it is not in season, 2 packages of frozen asparagus spears.

Salad, as you will.

Preparations

The previous evening put the sweetbreads to soak in a bowl of cold water that you can put in the refrigerator. Change the water before you go to bed.

The morning of your dinner blanch the sweetbreads by boiling them three minutes in unseasoned water. Return them to the refrigerator this time covered with a few tablespoonfuls of the water they cooked in to prevent their drying out.

At your convenience, when they are cool, pull or cut from them all the cartilage that feels hard to your touch, and shape them up as you want them to look when they are served, remembering if you seem to have a great deal of meat for two people that they will shrink considerably in cooking. When they are in shape, with your chef's knife cut the beef fat into ¼-inch slices; admittedly they may crack, but do the best you can to keep them whole, and likewise as you cut them again into strips ¼-inch square. In each sweetbread make a series of four holes crosswise through the soft meat; a clean screw driver well serves this purpose, or a small sharp knife: push the ¼-inch strips of beef fat into these holes, preferably so that the parts of the fat that obtrude on both sides are even; if the strips break, you can use several of them in the same hole to get this effect. This may seem unnecessary bother, and you can omit this larding if you will; but the sweetbreads will be better for it: the absolutely lean meat of the sweetbreads is best when in this way it is given some internal grease. If you are doing this well in advance, refrigerate the sweetbreads again.

If you are using fresh asparagus, cut from the stalk tips no longer than three inches: the stalks can be utilized in a cream of asparagus soup (see p. 146). Scrub each tip lightly with the vegetable brush under running cold water and leave the cleaned tips soaking in a bowl of cold water. The short frozen spears need no preparation.

Cooking

50 minutes

Grate an onion and a carrot through the medium grater. Start a few fragments of the beef fat simmering in a saucepan with a removable handle that you can put in the oven; as it yields its fat, fry in it the grated carrots and onion, seasoning it with 5 stalks of parsley, ½ teaspoonful of salt, ten grinds on the pepper grinder, ¼ teaspoonful of thyme, and ¼ teaspoonful of marjoram.

45 minutes

Start the oven to bring it to 350°. Lay the larded sweetbreads on this bed of seasonings by now well fried, and hence yielding their maximum flavor; pour over them a can of beef consommé, and bring to a boil.

40 minutes

Remove the handle of the saucepan and put the saucepan in the 350° oven to continue its cooking.

20 minutes

Start toward a boil water in a saucepan your steamer will fit.

15 minutes

Start steaming the asparagus tips. Set to soften 2 teaspoonfuls of arrowroot flour in ¼ cup of white wine.

10 minutes

Remove the saucepan from the oven and remove from it the sweetbreads which should now be dark brown and glazed; keep them warm on the platter on which you wish to serve them in the unlighted oven with the door open. Strain off the liquid from the seasonings into a small saucepan through a fine sieve; if there should be too little to make as much sauce as you want, add consommé. Thicken what should be a relatively clear brown sauce with the wine and arrowroot flour. Pour a little of it over the sweetbreads on the platter, to glaze them further; put the rest in a bowl to serve apart.

To serve, arrange the asparagus tips around the sweetbreads on their platter, arranging some of them in fans at the platter's ends. The asparagus needs no butter: the sauce serves it as well as the sweetbreads.

An agreeable preliminary to this meal (and the sweetbreads and the asparagus can wait while you enjoy it) would be the marinated mushrooms described on p. 141. If strawberries and pineapples are in season, the combination of them suggested on p. 185 would provide a congenial dessert.

This meal calls for a light red wine.

Menu 29

Braised Short Ribs of Beef   Carrots   Onions

Dinner for two

A SECOND classic form of braising, with a cut of beef that responds well to it.

Shopping list

2 short ribs of beef: the better the butcher, the better the short ribs, because better butchers are likely to have cut them from a rib roast of big beef that was someone else's extravagance.

If you can find it, buy also one calf's foot, and ask the butcher to cut it into three or four pieces to open up its cartilage.

1 lb. of white-skinned onions.

1 small can of tiny carrots.

Salad, as you will

Preparations

Peel the small onions and leave them soaking in water for later use.

Slice in ½-inch slices a fresh carrot and a medium-sized onion.

Wash and dry the salad; make the salad dressing.

Cooking

3½ hours

Put the short ribs in a saucepan with a removable handle and, starting the oven, put them in it for fifteen minutes to brown and yield some of their fat; don't allow the oven heat to exceed 400°.

3¼ hours

Remove the saucepan from the oven and establish it over moderate heat on the top of the stove. Fry the sliced onions and carrots in the grease the short ribs have by now yielded, not letting them brown. Deglaze the pan with 2 cups of white wine; its inclusion may seem to make braising costly; the results are well worth it. Add a can of beef consommé, 5 stalks of parsley, ¼ teaspoonful of thyme, ¼ teaspoonful of marjoram, 1 teaspoonful of salt, and ten grinds on the pepper grinder. If you found a calf's foot, add it at this point. Reduce the heat to the lowest possible and leave simmering for three hours.

20 minutes

Put the peeled small onions into the broth of the braise to cook in it and to add their flavor to it.

10 minutes

Open the can of tiny carrots, drain off their water, and add them to the broth. Set to soften 1 tablespoonful of arrowroot flour in ¼ cup of white wine.

5 minutes

With a perforated spoon remove from the broth the short ribs and put them on the platter on which you wish to serve them; similarly remove the small onions and the carrots, and arrange them round the short ribs. Strain the sauce into a small saucepan through a fine sieve; thicken it to a clear brown sauce with the wine and arrowroot flour; pour a little of it over the short ribs and the vegetables, and serve the rest apart in a bowl. The French also serve the pieces of calf's foot; I throw them away; they've served their purpose.

This is a dish that can be kept warm till you want it, so that you could enjoy a *potage* of water cress (see p. 148) as a preliminary. For dessert, try Imperial Pears (see p. 189).

This meal calls for a full red wine.

I said at the outset that short ribs responded well to braising because with their interspersed fat they are already larded. This procedure is precisely that of Beef à la Mode. This classic dish is difficult in this country only because the tender, lean meat used for it in France, like the lean meat of sweetbreads, needs the internal grease that larding provides. In France this can be readily procured at any butcher's. But in the United States most butchers think it enough to wrap a "pot roast" in thin sheets of pork fat. If you can find some butcher who will really lard a choice cut of beef, cook it in this way, and you will have the classic *Boeuf à la mode*. "Really larding" means piercing the meat with strips of fat, using a larding needle; "a choice cut" means . . . I must confess I have never been able to translate the French cuts of beef into their English equivalents. As to cut, the only recourse I know is to depend on your butcher—and to persuade him to lard the cut he regards as best.

If short ribs, as here suggested, are the cut, there will be no meat left over: it is virtually sure to be all eaten. If any of the sauce is left, treasure it for other uses; essentially it is a fine, clear brown sauce.

If your butcher supplies you a choice cut for a "pot roast," there may be some meat left over. If so, cherish both it, its sauce, and any leftover carrots and onions. If you had a calf's foot in the broth, it will jelly of itself; if not, you can make it jell by adding to the sauce 2 teaspoonfuls of unflavored gelatin softened in ¼ cup of white wine, heating the sauce till the gelatin is dissolved. Slice the remaining meat neatly into ½-inch slices; arrange them and any remaining carrots and onions in a Pyrex pie plate and pour over them the gelatinous sauce. Refrigerate, and you have a second meal, which some prefer to the first, *Boeuf à la mode en gelée*.

Menu 30

Braised Ham   Celery Mornay   Mousse of Chocolate

Buffet for ten to fifteen

Braising in its full classic form that produces a handsome ham as the central dish for a buffet meal, in this first version hot, but readily converted, with a few minor adaptations noted below, into a cold buffet. Complicated as it may seem on first reading, it is a meal that calls for a minimum of last-minute activity in its hot version, none in its cold version. Its secret, of course, is advance preparation. Thus in either version it is best attempted when you have a free day, say a Saturday, though its preparation need take up only a part of your time.

Shopping list

In the case of this meal your shopping should be done the day before.

1 whole ham. An eight-pound ham, if you can find one so small, will serve ten people, a ten-pound ham, fifteen, with some left over in both cases. Most hams are now more or less precooked, except for those of the Virginia type, by hot smoking. For the best braised ham, avoid those that are precooked to the point of being labeled "ready to serve," and in general be guided by the cooking time usually indicated on the wrapper. My preference is for the leaner, harder hams, with true Virginia hams ruled out only by their cost; recently I have been relying on a lean ham from North Carolina.

4 to 6 bunches of celery, depending on how many inner tender stalks each will yield.

½ lb. mushrooms.

¼ lb. of Swiss cheese.

1 package of unsweetened chocolate in ounce squares: you will use four squares.

1 lb. of confectioners' sugar.

1 pint of sour cream.

1 lb. of *petits fours*, assorted cookies, from the best French bakery you know.

Preparations

The evening before your dinner put the ham to soak in water in the roasting pan; turn it and change the water before you go to bed.

The morning before your dinner prepare first the seasonings for braising: grate through the medium grater 4 carrots, similarly grate 2 peeled onions, slice one outside stalk of celery, leaves and all, twenty grinds on the pepper grinder, ½ teaspoonful of thyme, ½ teaspoonful of marjoram, 1 bay leaf, 4 whole cloves, and 10 stalks of parsley.

If the ham is still in its skin, remove it, which you can do readily with your sharp chef's knife: insert its point under the skin at the butt end, pressing the cutting edge against the tough, uncuttable skin to avoid shearing off more than a minimum of the underlying white fat; when in this way you have loosened enough skin to grip, hold it up firmly with your left hand, continuing with the knife in your right hand to cut against the growing flap as you peel it back. Trim off any remaining skin or darkened surfaces of the fat so that in the end all the fat is gleaming white. Retain some of the fat parings for later use.

Put the seasonings in the bottom of the roasting pan, lay the ham on them, and pour over it 1 cup of marsala (or sherry) or even 2 cups, if you can bring yourself to splurge. Cover the pan (if it has no cover, you can seal it in with a broad sheet of aluminum foil), and leave the ham to absorb these flavors.

Start to boil a large saucepan of water to which is added 1 10½-ounce can of beef consommé. Wash and dry the inner tenderer stalks of the celery and cut them (four or five at a time) crossways into ¼-inch slices. When the water and consommé mixture comes to a boil, put the celery slices in it and simmer for an hour, adding water if necessary, but no more than will boil away in an hour's simmering. When the celery is cooked and virtually dry, pour it into a baking dish (I use an oversized cocotte) in which you will serve it. Cover and set aside for later use.

Make a quart of white sauce (see p. 154) and as it thickens grate and melt into it ¼ pound of Swiss cheese; salt to taste, probably with 2 teaspoonfuls of salt; if the weather is hot, it may be preferable to bottle and refrigerate this sauce; if it is reasonably cool, it can remain in its double boiler till evening.

Remove the stems from ½ pound of mushrooms, wash the heads and slice them crosswise in ⅛-inch slices. Refrigerate for later use.

Prepare the mousse of chocolate. In a large double boiler top over hot water on brisk heat melt 4 ounce squares of unsweetened chocolate into 1 cup of confectioners' sugar, and 1 cubic inch of butter, flavored with 2 inches from a vanilla bean, to yield a smooth paste. Meanwhile, separate the yolks of 4 eggs from the whites (retaining the whites) into a small bowl and beat them till they turn a lighter yellow. Remove the double boiler top from the heat to the kitchen shelf and stir into the chocolate paste first 1 pint of sour cream, then the beaten egg yolks, and finally 1 teaspoonful of salt; remove the vanilla bean at this point. In a large clean bowl, having washed and carefully dried your egg beater, beat stiff the 4 egg whites; if a drop of water remains on your egg beater they will not stiffen. Pour onto the stiff whites the mixture from the double boiler top, and "fold" it into the beaten egg whites with a two-tined fork; this "folding" is essentially a large circular motion of the fork that gradually mixes in the whites without too much breaking down their fluffiness. Continue folding until the now-finished mousse is consistent in color, i.e., until no beaten egg white is visible. Pour the mousse into the bowl in which you wish to serve it; at this point the mixture will be fluid enough to settle with a flat top; refrigerate it to harden, and to avoid contamination cover it with a broad piece of aluminum foil.

This completes your preparations and leaves you free till actual cooking should begin.

Cooking

3½ hours

The timing here for braising the ham assumes a 9-pound ham, not precooked, which requires for baking (as for braising) twenty minutes to the pound. Start the oven to bring it to 350°. Lift the ham from its seasonings; strain the wine from them through a sieve into a bowl; put the roasting pan on direct heat on the top of the stove with some of the scraps of fat and parings you retained, and when they have yielded some of their grease, remove them; fry the seasonings in this grease, not allowing them to brown, to bring them to full flavor. Again lay the ham on them, pour over it the wine from the bowl and 2 10½-ounce cans of beef consommé; add enough water to bring the liquid to a third of the ham's height. Put it in the 350° oven to braise slowly. Except to be sure that it isn't cooking too fast, i.e., browning too rapidly, it needs no further attention for approximately two and a half hours. Nor need any further cooking be done till toward that time.

40 minutes

Rewarm the white sauce and cheese in its double boiler top and add to it the cooked celery slices, allowing whatever liquid remains in them slightly to thin the white sauce. Separate 3 egg yolks from their whites into a small bowl for later use; there is no present use for the whites.

30 minutes

Take the roasting pan from the oven and remove the ham from it; strain off into a saucepan through a sieve the liquid from the roasting pan; restore the ham to the roasting pan and sprinkle ½ cup of brown sugar as evenly as possible over its fat; reduce the oven heat to 300°, and return the ham to it to acquire the glaze on its fat that the brown sugar will produce; watch it from time to time to be sure that the sugar is not browning to a burn: should it, extinguish the oven heat, and leave the oven door open a few minutes so that the ham may remain there, warm, till you wish to serve it.

20 minutes

Simmer the liquid from the braising over moderate heat on the top of the stove, skimming off as much foam and fat as you can while it simmers. Set to soften 1 tablespoonful of arrowroot flour in ½ cup of marsala (or sherry). After several skimmings add to the sauce the mushroom slices.

If, as is likely at this point, your guests have begun to arrive for cocktails, your only present concern in the kitchen is that the ham should not be overbrowned. If you have already brought it to the desired glaze, and have cooled and shut off the oven, even that is no concern. You can hold this meal at this point easily for as much as half an hour, if necessary, even longer; the ham has been thoroughly heated through in its long cooking and in a merely warm oven will not cool; the celery is happy in its not quite finished sauce. If you can manage it, warm the baking dish in which you intend to serve the celery in the merely warm oven. Otherwise, you can forget your cooking for a time.

10 minutes

It need be resumed hardly more than before you wish to serve. Resuming it then, beat the 3 egg yolks till they turn a lighter yellow, dilute them with 1 tablespoonful of milk, and beat briefly again; stir them into the celery in its sauce for its final thickening, adding at the same time 1 cubic inch of butter.

5 minutes

Once more skimming the sauce from the braising, stir into it the arrowroot flour and sherry to thicken it to a clear brown sauce. Start the broiler.

To serve, put the ham on a proper platter or board. Pour the celery in what is now sauce Mornay into the warm (but not hot, lest its heat curdle the sauce) baking dish and briefly expose it to the preheated broiler, as close to the heat as possible, with the broiler door open so that you can watch it every second; expose it only until the surface of the sauce begins to spot with brown, the final touch for a dish with this sauce. Serve the sauce for the ham in a separate bowl.

These are two handsome dishes, and you should have given some thought to how you will display them to best advantage. For this meal I put the ham on one side of the dining table, with the plates on which it is to be served on the left, its sauce in the bowl to the right. The celery Mornay is well placed on the opposite side of the table, with its serving spoon, and the knives, forks, and napkins for each guest. As I carve and serve the ham on plates on my side of the table, I suggest that they serve the celery Mornay for themselves, as they pick up their knife, fork, and napkin on the other side.

A whole ham is best carved by starting with a vertical cut through the fat about three inches up from the leg bone; the successive cuts are more and more slanting, and the slices progressively bigger as carving proceeds; I usually set aside the first small slices for myself, and begin serving the guests only when the slices are somewhat larger.

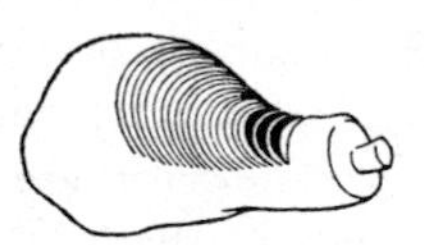

Carving a ham

Similarly, for this meal, I arrange the sideboard for the dessert service, with the plates, forks, and dessert spoons, *petits fours*, the coffee cups and coffee service, leaving a space in the middle to give the mousse of chocolate a proper display when it is brought in at dessert time.

Equally important with this number of guests is the state of the kitchen, and the state of your mind when the guests leave. Our procedure (for this is my wife's department!) is to have filled our largest soup kettle with a strong solution of detergent and water, and to have established it out of the way, so that plates as they come from the table can be slipped into it and thus can be more readily washed the following morning. Similarly, as I finished with the roasting pan I rinsed it out, and established it in the sink with its solution of water and detergent, to receive the silver as it has been used. In finishing the meal, also, I rinsed and set aside the only other two cooking dishes, the double boiler top and the saucepan. The other cooking dishes I had washed and put away as cooking proceeded, leaving the kitchen shelf free for glasses, etc. Usually we at least rinse the ham's platter and the celery's baking dish before going to bed. The remains of the ham are refrigerated wrapped in aluminum foil for subsequent uses. Thus the kitchen is relatively clear when the meal begins, and in not too bad a state when you go, I trust, happily to bed.

This meal already has its dessert. If it graces a real occasion, and you want a preliminary, nothing could be more appropriate than a green turtle soup served hot from the table from a soup tureen into cups. Excellent green turtle soup is now readily available in cans, or better still in quart jars in fish markets. It is usually improved by adding a generous amount of marsala (or sherry), say ½ cup to a quart at the last minute. If you want to economize with it, few of your guests will be aware that you have diluted it with beef consommé, which is, in any case, the stock of this soup.

You may also feel that you wish your buffet to include a salad. If so, this seems an occasion for a mixed green salad made up, for example, of the inner, crisp leaves of chicory, water cress, and lettuce. On such an occasion as this, guests are glad to serve themselves to it on their dinner plates. On the chance that someone is allergic to chocolate, and so cannot eat the mousse, and for those who like cheese with salad, it might be well to have a fine piece of Gorgonzola, the Italian blue cheese, on the dessert buffet.

This is a meal for a white wine throughout. If the occasion is really grand, it will support champagne.

If you wish to serve a cold rather than this hot buffet, only slight adaptations are called for.

Braise the ham the previous day, carrying it through to the final glazing, allowing it to cool, and refrigerating it to chill it thoroughly. Likewise chill the strained juice from the braising; when it is thoroughly chilled, its fat will have formed an easily removable top layer; remove it, and you will find the sauce jellied underneath. (Good cooks retain this highly seasoned fat for other uses, e.g., fried eggs at breakfast.) If you have approximately a quart of this jelly, and it is, as it is likely to be, of about the consistency of a jellied consommé, soften 3 teaspoonfuls of unflavored gelatin in ½ cup of marsala (or sherry), and when it is a paste add it to the jelly in a saucepan over moderate heat, and heat till the gelatin is dissolved. Pour this aspic into a baking tin and refrigerate it again. If the weather is hot, as it is likely to be when you want your buffet cold, several hours before serving establish the ham on the platter on which it is to be served; heating the pan in which is your aspic by dipping the pan briefly in hot water, turn the block of aspic out on a piece of aluminum foil, and with your chef's knife cut it into neat squares or diamonds. Lifting them with a spatula, arrange them on the platter's rim, and refrigerate it. Serve it thoroughly chilled, or even as I do in really hot weather, over a large baking pan of ice into which my platter just fits. In other words, in hot weather the fine sauce of this dish, like the ham, is served cold; and there is no finer cold ham than the one that has been braised.

For this cold buffet substitute for the hot celery Mornay the unusual *salade composée*, Salade Beaucaire (see p. 175). Naturally, modify your shopping list accordingly. It likewise should be prepared well in advance.

Thus this buffet, in its cold version, requires no last-minute preparations beyond bringing from the refrigerator to the table the fruits of earlier labor.

PART III

A LA CARTE

The preceding Thirty Menus—enough for the average month of good cooking—provide the basis of thirty well-planned meals, adequate in themselves. If your experience in the use of this book is like mine—and I have used it for more than two years before preparing this revised version—you will come to rely on them, as often in a restaurant you are happy and well-advised to follow the *carte du jour*. In following them, you can be sure, even when rushed or distracted, that your shopping list is complete, and that your meal will be on time.

But none of them carries the prohibition of poorer eating-houses, "No substitutions allowed." Furthermore, they only suggest a preliminary course and a dessert. Part III, "A la Carte," offers the variety good eating calls for in these respects, and finally, and most importantly, in building for yourself a meal that suits the moment's taste. Incidentally, as in the best of restaurants, it includes what are in my house, and may be in yours, *specialitiés de la maison*.

1. HORS D'OEUVRES

Hors d'oeuvres are by no means restricted to the usually tempting assortment of cold dishes presented in identical porcelain platters for one's choice, *hors d'oeuvres variés*, or *les crudités*, as they are now sometimes called in more pretentious French restaurants. Actually, the choicest hors d'oeuvres are best eaten by themselves with bread for contrast: *pâté de foie gras*, caviar, smoked salmon, or sturgeon, an egg in aspic—or even in French taste, a single component of *hors d'oeuvres variés*, such as thinly sliced salami or celery-root mayonnaise. Often, in the taste of the moment, an assortment of them may make an entire luncheon or supper—though traditionally they are a luncheon preliminary, with soup replacing them at night, as it is etymologically retained in the word supper. Etymologically, likewise, they are something outside the main preoccupation of the meal, something to sustain and even whet the appetite before the main dish appears.

If you are drawn to having them in their varied form, you need have no more than one component from each of the four main categories that follow (or from each of three, if one omits the eggs): fish, meat, and vegetables. For convenience, they are treated here in their variety, with those most worthy of appearing in solitary splendor marked with an asterisk. Nor are those identical porcelain platters essential for serving a variety; well arranged on a single platter, or on one with well-conceived divisions, they are quite as attractive. Such a platter might offer, for example, the contents of a fine can of sardines, a dozen slices, as thin as your delicatessen man's machine will slice them, of a hard Italian salami, neatly arranged slices of tomato over which you have poured sauce vinaigrette with its bright green parsley, celery cut crosswise in mayonnaise, with a couple of deviled eggs as centerpiece. The lists that follow indicate how wide the variety may be.

Fish

* *Anchovies*, best in olive oils from tins, preferably the thick filets, rather than the rolled variety; laid out on a slice of toast, they make in themselves an admirable preliminary.

* *Caviar*, preferably served alone, with its traditional accompaniments, the yolks and whites of hard-boiled eggs put separately through a not-too-fine sieve, and finely chopped onion or shallot, together with lemon pieces for additional flavor as desired. Caviar is still at its best in the Russian or Persian varieties from the Caspian. Good in flavor, but lacking in consistency are the German and Danish varieties that are now appearing in Europe. An undervalued variation is the fine red salmon caviar now generally available in the United States at moderate prices.

* *Herring*, at their best pickled (not cooked) in wine and spices, and procurable in this form in the United States in tins from the Scandinavian and Low Countries. A favorite variation is Bismark herring, the pickled fish in sour cream and onion slices.

* *Sardines*, in any good variety.

Shrimp, really worthy of being served alone only in their utmost freshness, and preferably whole in their entire shells, as in the *bouquet d'écrivisses* of the best European restaurants. The less tasteful American varieties probably require the tomato cocktail sauce or mayonnaise in which they customarily are served. Not to be disregarded are the small, even tiny, Scandinavian and Japanese shrimp now procurable in tins, or the tiny South American shrimp that can be bought in frozen blocks.

Smoked eel, procurable in tins, for most tastes better as a component than as a single dish.

* *Smoked salmon or sturgeon*, at its best served alone with pieces of lemon and when freshly sliced off in better delicatessen shops.

Smoked oysters or mussels, now readily procurable in the United States as an accompaniment to cocktails, but a real contribution to the hors d'oeuvres platter.

Meat

* *Ham*, your own left over, or what the delicatessen offers, but always sliced thin; a particularly fine variety is Italian *prosciutto*. A classic elaboration is such ham rolled into little cones (best in a conic

mold) and filled with ham paste such as can now be bought in tins; or in Italian style, rolled around pieces of fine sweet melon.

* *Pastes*, best of course true *pâté de foie gras*, served alone in slices with bread. Now also procurable are the American-made pastes of liver, ham, and chicken, which can be likewise served in slices if removed whole from the chilled can.

* *Sausages*, the whole range offered in delicatessen shops, salami, cervelat, bologna, liverwurst, with the hard varieties (like the first two) sliced as thin as the machine will slice them.

Vegetables

Apples, an unusual but admirable component for the hors d'oeuvres platter if cored, peeled, and sliced thin (as for a pie or tart) and then cooked three minutes in a thin syrup made of a tablespoonful each of sugar and curry powder; drain and serve cold.

Beets, the pickled variety readily obtainable in tins and jars.

Cabbage, in the well-known form of cole slaw, shredded in either mayonnaise or French dressing.

Celery, in thin crosswise slices in either mayonnaise or French dressing.

Celery root, (knob celery), served either grated or in the thin, two-inch-long pieces known as *juliennes*, in mayonnaise. (Celery root is now usually in the market most of the winter; the knob is simply washed, peeled, and grated or sliced).

Cucumbers, peel, slice thin, salt, and spread on a platter to give up their water; thirty minutes later drain it off, and serve the limp slices in a French dressing with chopped dill sprinkled over, or in chopped dill and sour cream. (If the water is not extracted under the influence of salt, your finished dish will be too watery.)

Eggplant, best and readiest in the canned Italian variety, *caponata*, or Eggplant Appetizer, found in almost any Italian grocery as an important component in *antipasti*, the Italian version of hors d'oeuvres.

Mushrooms, best when prepared as follows: wash and slice mushroom heads and boil for five minutes in salted water, drain, and boil again for ten minutes in ½ cup of white wine, ¼ cup of oil, a crushed clove of garlic, a little thyme, bay leaf, salt, and pepper; remove the slices, and reduce the broth by half for a sauce; serve cold in this sauce.

Olives, particularly in my taste the ripe varieties in oil sold in Italian and Greek shops.

Onions, the pickled varieties that you can readily find in delicatessen shops or in jars.

Pickles, a little-exploited American contribution to *haute cuisine,* particularly in the mixtures developed by American cooks: mustard pickles, piccalilli, watermelon pickles, etc.

Tomatoes, sliced thin in sauce Vinaigrette, sprinkled with extra parsley.

Eggs

Egg salad, hard-boiled eggs sliced crosswise or lengthwise in mayonnaise or sauce Rémoulade.

Deviled eggs, hard-boiled eggs whose yolks have been removed, crushed through a sieve, flavored with mayonnaise, mustard, curry, etc., and replaced in the whites.

* *Jellied eggs,* or eggs in aspic, poached eggs chilled in a mold in aspic, usually on a thin slice of ham. (See p. 180.)

In our household we find it agreeable and easy in the hot summer months to have a run on hors d'oeuvres which at that season, if followed say by good cheeses, provide a sufficient luncheon. For such "runs" we have accumulated a number of identical covered dishes which do equally well in the refrigerator and on the table. With such treatment, the components appear and reappear for several days, replaced, as one disappears, with another. For such a "run" it is well to slice the sausages and meats yourself, i.e., to get them in ½-pound pieces. Often, too, leftovers fit in, e.g., cold Shrimps Américaine.

Finally, there is one hors d'oeuvre which is for those that like them, *hors concours,* oysters. They are at their best, everywhere, just opened, on the half shell; but few will learn to open them (I have my scars), and now better fish shops will open them carefully, and so pack them that in carrying them home little of their juice and consequent freshness are lost. Not having crushed ice on which to serve them should be no deterrent: in the United States they are usually served too cold; American oysters, as contrasted with their European cousins, are at best delicate in flavor, and too much cold diminishes it. American oysters at their best–small, fresh, and from the best beds–may be eaten for themselves, as European oysters are best eaten. Ordinarily, they are best when served not too cold (merely kept in the refrigerator after you have brought them home) on a platter, where each guest with his fingers can take to his own plate and oyster fork as many as he wants. American oysters usually benefit from some added flavor, a dash of lemon, a bit of horse-radish, a ketchup to which lemon and horse-radish have been added, Tabasco sauce, or another that is usually disregarded: a tablespoonful of chopped shallots or onion in ¼ cup of vinegar, with a ¼ teaspoonful of salt and ten grinds on the pepper grinder. Any oyster, American or otherwise, is best accompanied by ⅛-inch slices of brown bread, e.g., the thin-sliced dark brown pumpernickel that you can now buy in most delicatessen shops, thinly spread with softened butter and cut in two for convenience in eating.

2. SOUPS

This section will deal mainly with the thick, or cream, soups, for several reasons. First, when well made, they are among the greatest in *haute cuisine*. Second, they are easily made, and often of materials that would otherwise go to waste. Third, even with the improvements that have been made in the canned varieties, they are to my taste better when made at home, of fresh and the best ingredients.

As remarked earlier, as a "cooking fool," I have from time to time tried my hand at the clear soups based on different meat stocks. But those stocks are not easy to make: most of them require eight hours' cooking with constant skimming; furthermore, the best ingredients for them, lean beef, veal, chicken, beef, and veal bones, and calves' feet, are by no means inexpensive. And clarifying the final product with egg whites and lean beef is at best a messy business. One that is relatively easy, inexpensive, and seldom so good as when made at home, ox-tail soup, I still make, and have included in Menu 20 so that you may make and enjoy it. In general, despite the objections of purist friends, I cling to the contention that the clear soups now readily obtainable in cans, consommés based on beef and chicken (not as yet on veal), and their variants, e.g., the tomato-flavored consommés generally known as madrilenes, are as good if not better than what can be made at home. For better or for worse, then, this book relies on them both for the stocks its recipes call for and for such clear soups as you may want.

For a meal that calls for a clear soup, I suggest using the canned varieties without dilution (if it is called for) and brightening them by garnishing. For example, a clear beef consommé is brightened by the addition ten minutes before serving of a few green peas, which in ten minutes' cooking will remain bright green; by some chopped fresh tarragon (when in season) or a slice of tomato added just before serving; for some, by a slice of lemon. Clear chicken consommé is similarly brightened by finely chopped parsley added at the last moment. One of the finest of clear soups, (suggested for Menu 30) green turtle soup, is also readily procurable in cans, or, better, in some fish markets, concentrated in glass jars, and extensible for reasons of economy by the addition of beef consommé: classic green turtle soup always includes beef stock.

In classic cookery most cream soups are based on prepared white sauce, béchamel (see below, p. 154); and when you have it on hand, as you not infrequently will, you, too, can prepare them in this way: simply simmer the flavoring ingredient, e.g., shredded mushroom stems, in white sauce in a double boiler top for half an hour, purée through the Foley Food Mill, garnish with slices of the flavoring ingredient, add a little cream, and serve. But you will not always have white sauce on hand, and in some instances its flavoring of carrots, onions, herbs, and spices is less happy in soups with the delicacy of chestnuts than in its other uses. Accordingly, there follows a procedure by which you can prepare a fine cream soup in as little as thirty minutes, though it will gain from longer simmering when time allows.

Suppose you find yourself with the stems of a pound of mushrooms and four or so mushroom heads which you prudently set aside with cream of mushroom soup in view.

30 minutes

Cook in the top of a double boiler a white *roux* composed of 2 cubic inches of butter and 2 tablespoonfuls of flour.

25 minutes

Wash the mushroom stems and shred them with your fingers; fry them three minutes in ½ cubic inch of butter, and remove them with a perforated spoon. Fry in the same butter the sliced mushroom caps and set them aside in the pan. In both instances, season with ½ teaspoonful of salt and five grinds on the pepper grinder.

15 minutes

Into the now cooked *roux* in the double boiler top pour 3 cups of cold milk and 1 cup of consommé, beef or chicken. Add the fried mushroom stems, and stir constantly till the soup thickens. If it is thicker than you want it, add more milk and consommé in the same proportions.

5 minutes

Put the soup through the Foley Food Mill, puréeing the mushroom stems and, incidentally, eliminating any lumpiness.

o minutes

Return the puréed soup to the double boiler top, adding the fried mushroom slices as a garnish. Salt to taste, and finish with a little cream. If the soup is for early use, it may simply be kept warm in the double boiler. If for later use, it can be poured off into hot Ball jars, and refrigerated, to be warmed before serving in the double boiler.

Similar cream soups which seem to me particularly rewarding are made of the following vegetables:

Cream of Corn: simply add a can of cream corn to the white sauce; it need not be, though I prefer it, puréed; garnish with ¼-inch squares of white bread fried brown in 1 cubic inch of butter or vegetable fat.

Cream of Peas: best made from a package of frozen peas added to the white sauce and puréed; a few can be boiled separately for garnish; or again the soup is well garnished with fried bread squares.

Cream of Celery: cut the outside stalks of celery in ½-inch slices crosswise, fry them for three minutes in ½ cubic inch of butter, add to the white sauce and presently purée; garnish with ⅛-inch slices of the inside tender stalks added five minutes before serving.

Cream of Asparagus: the lower parts of the stalks, not the tough bottoms, cut in 1-inch pieces are used in the white sauce, and the puréed soup is garnished with the tips, briefly fried in 1 cubic inch of butter.

Cream of Chestnuts: readily made of leftover chestnut purée, added to unflavored white sauce, and puréed again to avoid any lumpiness—a delicate and unusually delicious soup of this kind.

The same process yields a series of cream soups flavored with chicken or sea food.

Cream of Chicken à la Reine: at a chicken-in-pieces shop buy one breast. With a sharp knife peel off the raw white meat from the bone; cut it raw into ½-inch squares, setting aside for garnish those which turn out regular in shape, adding the others, together with the skin and the bone, to the cream sauce; simmer for at least an hour. Remove the bone and the skin, and purée the rest. Half an hour before serving add the regularly shaped squares for a garnish. Finish with ¼ cup of cream.

Cream of Shrimp: while preparing the cream sauce, fry ½ pound of shrimp in 1 cubic inch of butter with 1 tablespoonful each of finely chopped carrots, onions, and parsley stems; reserve six or more for a garnish. Season with 1 teaspoonful of salt and five grinds on the pepper grinder. Deglaze the frying pan with ¼ of a cup of white wine (or, for stronger flavor, sherry) and add to the white sauce to simmer for at least half an hour; purée, garnish with the shrimp you set aside; finish with ¼ cup of cream.

Cream of Oysters: poach a dozen shelled-out oysters by bringing them to a boil in their own juice; set 4 aside whole for garnish; cut the remaining 8 in four pieces each and add to the cream sauce; simmer for thirty minutes and purée; not more than five minutes before serving add the whole oysters (they will be tough if cooked longer), finish with ¼ cup of cream.

Another series of thick soups, called *potages* rather than *crêmes* in French, is worth noting both for themselves and because, served cold, they yield a favorite American cold soup, not found in the French cookbooks as such, Vichyssoise. Though this series takes somewhat longer to prepare, the basic component of it, leek and potato purée, when once prepared can be kept for some days, even as much as a week, in Ball jars under refrigeration.

2 hours

Wash and slice crosswise in ¼-inch slices the tender parts of 3 leeks (or if you cannot find them, 3 onions). Peel and cut into ½-inch squares 1 pound of potatoes, keeping the pieces in cold water to avoid their turning brown.

1 hour, 50 minutes

Fry the slices of leeks (or onions) in 2 cubic inches of butter until they are about to brown; drain off the water from the potato pieces and add them to the leeks and fry them, again without letting them brown.

1¾ hours

Sprinkle 2 tablespoonfuls of flour over the vegetables, stirring constantly, in effect to make a *roux* of the flour and the butter in the pan.

1 hour, 40 minutes

Cover the vegetables with 2 quarts of liquid, water, and chicken consommé, preferably half and half. Let simmer for approximately an hour and a half, adding water as needed to maintain about the same total volume.

Purée through the Foley Food Mill. *10 minutes*

Reheat for bottling as a basic component. ***5 minutes***

0 minutes

Pour off into Ball jars which you have preheated and more or less sterilized with boiling water.

This basic component yields a variety of soups.

Potage Parmentier: warm a pint of the basic component in the top of a double boiler; dilute with whole milk until it is somewhat thinner than you wish it to be when you serve it; five minutes before serving finish with a beaten egg yolk diluted after beating with 1 tablespoonful of cream; garnish with tiny fried bread squares. Salt to taste.

Potage of Water Cress: warm a pint of the basic component in a saucepan; dilute with milk to the thickness you wish it to be when served; ten minutes before serving, add the finely chopped leaves of a bunch of water cress. Salt to taste and finish with a ¼ cup of cream.

Vichyssoise: in a mixing bowl dilute a pint of the basic component with half a pint of cream and as much more whole milk as is needed to yield the thickness you prefer. Salt, and flavor cautiously with Worcestershire sauce, not more than 1 teaspoonful. Rebottle in a quart jar, refrigerate. It can be brought back to a creamy cold soup by vigorous shaking just before serving. Garnish each serving with a teaspoonful of finely chopped chives.

Another soup, surprisingly simple to make, that deserves honorable mention here is onion soup:

Peel and slice 2 medium-sized onions into ½-inch slices, and then again at ½-inch intervals across the slices, to yield what are approximately ½-inch squares. Fry them in 1 cubic inch of butter in a saucepan over low to moderate heat, stirring them constantly till they are golden brown. Add 1 teaspoonful of salt and ten grinds on the pepper grinder. The soup can be finished by adding 1 quart of water and simmering it for ten minutes more. It will be richer if you include 1 10½-ounce can of beef consommé in the water. Traditionally, it is served with thin rounds of French bread sprinkled with grated spaghetti cheese. In the best practice the soup is put in some serving dish that resists oven heat (e.g., your large cocotte) in a 350° or even 400° oven till these croutons, floating with their cheese on its surface, brown.

Two other somewhat unorthodox soups, both of them *specialités de ma maison,* deserve inclusion, the first another neglected cold soup, the second a great regional dish of Maine. Both depend on leftovers.

When you have leftover curry of chicken (Menu 23) in summer, you can enjoy it in cold cream of curry:

Remove the chicken meat from any remaining bone with your fingers; well cooked as it is, it should shred off easily. Put the meat and the sauce in a saucepan, dilute with a pint of milk, and simmer fifteen minutes. Purée the mixture through the Foley Food Mill and refrigerate in Ball jars preheated with boiling water. To prepare for serving, mix with as much cream as is needed to bring it to the proper thickness in a larger jar, and chill; restore it to creaminess by shaking vigorously just before serving.

When you have eaten lobsters for themselves, i.e., simply boiled, hot or cold, you are ready for lobster stew:

Simply retain all the debris. I usually serve lobsters shelled, and as I shell them in the kitchen, put the shells and such watery juice as comes from them in a large soup pot together with the coral (eggs) from female lobsters and the green tamale from both sexes (unless I have a guest who savors it, and sometimes even then on the sly). As soon as possible, at least right after the meal, fry these shells in at least 2 cubic inches of butter, stirring them from time to time with a stout spoon. When the watery juice has fried away, and you have what appears to be (and is) a thick, buttery glaze on the bottom of the pot, pour in ¼ cup of whisky (or, if you prefer and can afford it, of brandy: whisky is the Maine ingredient), and as it steams up, light it with a match. Keep it flaming as long as you can by shaking the pot. Cover the shells with whole milk, with probably 2 quarts being required, and simmer, without allowing it to come to a full boil, for at least an hour, preferably two. Strain the liquid from the shells through a coarse sieve or colander, and bottle in Ball jars preheated with boiling water. Refrigerate for use the next day. To serve, simply warm in the top of a double boiler, garnishing it with any pieces of cooked lobster meat you were able to salvage from the lobster meal. To provide it, I often hold out from my guests the "arms," the section of the lobster between the body and the claws proper, which yield good chunks of firm meat.

Such a lobster stew is hardly a soup, but a meal—a luncheon or a supper in itself. Strained through a coarse sieve or colander, it will be somewhat thickened by minute particles of lobster meat and colored by the basic butter reddened by the coral. (Incidentally, this colored fat will rise to the top of the refrigerated bottles and should be retained when the stew is warmed for serving.) If the stew is to serve by itself as a luncheon or a supper, a fine accompaniment is corn bread, readily made by baking corn-muffin mix in a flat baking pan.

3. SAUCES

In good cookery there are several basic sauces which may be and usually are prepared well in advance; one or the other of them has occasionally been called for in the preceding thirty menus, as, for example, clear brown sauce in the veal chasseur of Menu 26. If one agrees, as I do, to use canned stocks, e.g., beef or chicken consommé, they are surprisingly easy to prepare, and can even be readily prepared during actual cooking time. If, however, I foresee using one, it is generally easier to have it ready. If you make it well in advance, or, as often happens, have some left over, it keeps well in the refrigerator if bottled boiling into Ball jars, preheated, and more or less sterilized with boiling water.

Seldom are the basic sauces served by themselves, though one of them, white sauce (béchamel) may be, as with the radishes béchamel noted below (see p. 154). Rather they ordinarily figure as a component in a sauce that develops out of a particular dish (as in Veal Chasseur), or, more importantly, in sauces that are derived from them. There follow easy procedures for the preparation of each of these four basic sauces—brown sauce, clear brown sauce, velvet, and white sauce—with similar procedures for preparing some of the more interesting sauces that are derived from them, together with brief indications of dishes which they adorn.

Brown Sauce

Make the thickening (known as brown *roux*) in a small saucepan with a removable handle. On the top of the stove over medium heat brown deep brown 2 cubic inches of butter: the butter will melt, foam up, and then, if constantly stirred, will fall to a rich mahogany-brown liquid; don't be timid, brown the butter dark brown. Turn off the heat, add and stir into it 2 tablespoonfuls of flour until it forms a now light-brownish paste. Remove the handle of the pan and put it in a 300° oven; watch it, and stir it occasionally, until the paste has returned to the first mahogany color of the browned butter; again don't be timid: bake the *roux* till it is really dark. Restoring the handle of the pan, add to it on the top of the stove over moderate heat 1 10½-ounce can of beef consommé, stirring the *roux* into it and skimming off any light foam that may develop as it comes to a boil. Leave it simmering five minutes. The resulting sauce will not be so thick as you might have expected from the 2 tablespoonfuls of flour that went into it, for the reason that the flour has already been partially cooked. Thus the resulting sauce should not be *floury* in the adverse sense of the term, but rather smooth and limpid.

From Brown Sauce

Sauce Poivrade: the classic accompaniment for red-meated game, e.g., venison, but good with goose, turkey, or even beefsteak, if game isn't handy. Fry in 1 cubic inch of butter 1 grated carrot, 1 grated onion, 3 tablespoonfuls of chopped parsley stems, a little thyme and bay leaf. Add ¼ cup of vinegar, ¼ cup of white wine, and boil till the liquid is reduced by one half. Add a pint of brown sauce and let the mixture simmer at least half an hour. Then add 10 crushed peppercorns (you can easily crush them in a small bowl by pounding them with a pestle, or lacking it by pressing hard on them with the bowl of a teaspoon under your thumb: they should be merely crushed, not powdered, so that the pieces later will not go through the sieve). Cook the sauce with the pepper pieces not more than ten minutes, to avoid too much predominance of the pepper flavor. Finish by straining through the Foley Food Mill, not to force through the solid materials, but simply to extract their juice.

Sauce Piquante: particularly good with pork and beef tongue. Chop or grate finely 3 tablespoonfuls of shallots or onions and boil them in ¼ cup each of vinegar and white wine until the liquid has almost disappeared, i.e., till the result is a thick paste of onion. Pour in 1 pint of brown sauce and simmer for ten minutes, skimming off any foam that develops. Prepare to add, at the last, 2 tablespoonfuls each of finely grated sweet gherkins and parsley and as much tarragon if you can muster it; add these ingredients at the last minute to conserve their greenness.

Clear Brown Sauce

This is a sauce on which you will come to rely more and more for its simplicity in preparation and its purity of flavor. Start toward a boil in a small saucepan 1 10½-ounce can of beef consommé. Set to soften in ¼ cup of white wine 2 teaspoonfuls of arrowroot flour. (If you cannot find arrowroot flour, cornstarch or potato flour will do, but barely.) After a minute stir the arrowroot flour and the wine and add the mixture to the warming consommé. As it comes to a boil, it will turn into a clear sauce that will catch you, happily, in the nostrils.

From Clear Brown Sauce

Sauce Madère: particularly good with ham or tongue. Simply add to clear brown sauce just before serving ¼ cup of one of the strong wines, madeira, by definition, but marsala, port, or even a rich sherry will serve quite as well. If you wish this sauce garnished with raisins (as in Menu 24) add them when you begin to warm the sauce; another engaging garnish is the small white seedless grapes.

Sauce Robert: the sauce in which it is said you can readily eat your grandmother, at its best ordinarily (without pejorative implications) with pork. Fry without browning in 1 cubic inch of butter 1 finely grated onion. Add ¼ cup of white wine and boil till the wine has almost disappeared, i.e., till the result is a thick paste of onion. Add 1 pint of clear sauce, and simmer ten minutes, skimming off any foam that develops. This sauce may be strained through the Foley Food Mill or not, as you prefer. Finish by adding ½ teaspoonful of sugar and 1 tablespoonful of dry mustard, after which it should not be allowed to boil again.

Velvet (from meat stock)

Cook together in the top of a double boiler over hot water 2 cubic inches of butter and 2 tablespoonfuls of flour to make a white *roux*. After at least fifteen minutes' cooking add approximately 1 pint of stock (beef or chicken consommé, for example) to produce a smooth, velvety sauce. If you want this sauce thicker, it can be further thickened by reducing it in boiling it over direct heat.

Velvet (chicken stock)

Sauce Suprême: simmer the shredded stems of ½ pound of mushrooms in 1 10-ounce can of chicken consommé for at least half an hour. Strain off the resulting broth into 1 pint of chicken velvet, and boil over a direct flame till the sauce has reduced to one third of its original volume. Add ½ cup of thick sweet cream and continue boiling, but over a gentler flame, till the sauce clings to the spoon. Finish with 1 cubic inch of butter.

Sauce Estragon: whenever you can procure fresh tarragon, chop enough to yield at least 1 tablespoonful, and boil it in ¼ cup of white wine till the liquid has almost disappeared. Add the resulting paste to 1 pint of chicken velvet in a double boiler. To finish, add ¼ cup of thick, sweet cream and 1 cubic inch of butter. At the last moment add another tablespoonful of chopped tarragon.

Velvet (from fish stock)

This velvet is made precisely as the meat velvets, except that you must prepare its stock, *fumet* (or scent) of fish, as it is best made with bits of the fish whose sauce it is to grace, i.e., any delicate white fish, like sole. Boil its trimmings gently for half an hour in 3 cups of water, 1 cup of white wine, 1 sliced onion, 5 stalks of parsley, a bare ⅛ teaspoonful of thyme, a bare ⅛ teaspoonful of marjoram, 5 grinds on the pepper grinder, and ½ teaspoonful of salt. Strain off the resulting broth into white *roux* cooked for at least fifteen minutes in a double-boiler top, and cook till thickening ceases.

From Fish Velvet

White Wine Sauce: warm a pint of fish velvet in the top of a double boiler. Beat the yolks of 2 eggs till they turn a lighter yellow and dilute with 1 tablespoonful of cream. Stir the egg yolks into the velvet, as they thicken it. Finish with 1 cubic inch of butter.

You may sometime wish to try what is really a variant of this sauce:

Sauce Normande: simmer for at least half an hour the shredded stems of ½ pound of mushrooms in 1 cup of fish stock. Strain off the resulting broth into 1 pint of fish velvet in the top of a double boiler. Beat the yolks of 2 eggs till they are a lighter yellow and dilute with 1 tablespoonful of cream. Stir the egg yolks into the velvet, as they thicken it. Season with the juice of half a lemon, and finish with ¼ cup of thick, sweet cream and 1 cubic inch of butter.

White Sauce (Béchamel)

Cook together in the top of a double boiler over hot water 2 cubic inches of butter and 2 tablespoonfuls of flour for at least fifteen minutes. At the same time simmer over low heat 1 pint of milk flavored with 1 sliced onion, 1 sliced carrot, 1 sliced stalk of celery (if you happen to have one), 5 stalks of parsley, ⅛ teaspoonful of thyme, ⅛ teaspoonful of marjoram, 1 bay leaf, 5 gratings of nutmeg on the nutmeg grater, 10 grinds on the pepper grinder. (I omit salt at this point, since it seems preferable to salt this sauce when you use it.) After at least fifteen minutes' simmering strain the flavored milk into the white *roux* in the double boiler top and cook the sauce till thickening has ceased, stirring it vigorously at first to mix the *roux* into the hot milk. As it thickens, add ½ a can (5 ounces) of beef or chicken consommé. If the sauce should show lumps of undissolved *roux*, as for all your stirring it occasionally will, strain it through the Foley Food Mill.

From White Sauce

Sauce Mornay: good with almost anything white or green, e.g., chicken or broccoli. Add ¼ cup of grated cheese, preferably grated Italian cheese for spaghetti, to 1 pint of white sauce and warm in the top of a double boiler; if the mixture when warm is thicker than a thick soup, dilute with milk. Beat the yolks of 2 eggs and dilute with 1 tablespoonful of milk. Ten minutes before serving add the egg yolks to the sauce, stirring frequently, and keeping the heat as low as possible to minimize the risk of curdling. Finish with 1 cubic inch of butter. Usually this sauce is poured over whatever it is to be served with in a heat-resistant dish, which is then placed for seconds under a hot broiler flame to allow its surface to take on the spots of brown that characterize it in its perfection.

Two other sauces, not properly basic sauces, should be included here, hollandaise sauce and mayonnaise, and their derivatives.

Hollandaise Sauce

Extract the juice of 1 lemon and add to it enough white vinegar, preferably white wine vinegar, to yield ¼ cup, and then an equal amount of water to yield ½ cup. In the top of a double boiler directly over the heat bring this ½ cup of liquid, seasoned by ten grinds on the pepper grinder, to a boil, and leave it boiling till it has reduced to 2 tablespoonfuls. (If by inadvertence it reduced further to a glaze, you can bring it back by the addition of 2 tablespoonfuls of water and brief boiling.) Separate 2 egg yolks from their whites and put them into a small bowl. Put the double boiler top with its reduced lemon juice and vinegar in the double boiler bottom and bring the water in the bottom to a brisk boil. Meanwhile, beat the 2 egg yolks till they turn a lighter yellow. Move the double boiler with boiling water in its bottom to the kitchen shelf, there to stay for the remainder of this process, and pour the seasoning mixture from its top into the beaten egg yolks; beat them briefly and pour them back into the double boiler top over the hot water in its bottom. Stir steadily with a wooden spoon, as the seasoned egg yolks thicken, and, to smooth and thin them a bit, add to them 1 tablespoonful of hot water from the bottom of the double boiler. Stirring steadily, add cold butter from the refrigerator 1 cubic inch at a time, till you have added 3 cubic inches; enough butter has been added when the hot sauce is the consistency of mayonnaise. Finally stir in ½ teaspoonful of salt. Hollandaise is a sauce that can curdle both in the making and if kept warm. By following this procedure I have not had any curdle for more than ten years. Note that the secret of its not curdling seems to be a minimum of heat and an occasional stirring; hence making it over water that has just boiled but is falling from boiling heat. In my experience it can be kept warm enough for fifteen minutes, if left over this cooling water and occasionally stirred. It is liable to curdle if you attempt to warm it by again heating the water under it, or even if you pour it into a too-hot serving bowl. I think adding the salt last is another precaution; but it may be a mere superstition on my part. If curdling does occur, and by this procedure it should not, you can sometimes again emulsify the sauce by adding another beaten egg yolk.

From Hollandaise

Sauce Béarnaise: a variant of Hollandaise in two ways. First, in the flavoring which is reduced in the top of the double boiler before the beaten egg yolks are added: to the lemon juice and vinegar is added the flavor of tarragon most simply by substituting tarragon vinegar, but better by adding tarragon stems (which are, of course, removed before the sauce is made); a further addition, if you wish, are 1 tablespoonful of finely chopped shallots or onions. Second, the sauce is finished with chopped tarragon added at the last moment, together with chopped parsley, if you are short of tarragon, to yield a bright yellow sauce with the contrasting green of the chopped herbs. The resulting sauce is a distinct addition to principal components as varied as beefsteak, salmon, or poached eggs.

Sauce Mousseline: simply Hollandaise to which is added in time to warm before serving a relatively small quantity of whipped cream, ¼ cup in volume for a serving for two people. It is particularly good with asparagus, broccoli, or, surprisingly, with shad roe.

Mayonnaise Sauce

Preferably, but not necessarily, before making this sauce, set the olive oil from which it is to be made in the refrigerator to cool; if you leave it there too long it will turn temporarily cloudy. When you are ready to make the sauce, put ice in your larger beating bowl and set inside it your smaller beating bowl. Separate into the smaller bowl the yolks of 2 eggs. (You have no further use for their whites.) Prepare ¼ cup of lemon juice and white vinegar, approximately half and half. Beat the egg yolks till they turn a lighter yellow, beating into them 1 teaspoonful of dry mustard and a dash of cayenne pepper. Pour out 1 cup of the chilled olive oil and, beating steadily add it, ⅛ cup at a time (not necessarily in drops, as is often advised) to the beaten egg yolks. If you have the steady beating of an electric beater, you can be virtually sure that the yolks and the oil will immediately and progressively emulsify to produce a sauce that already looks like mayonnaise. If, inexplicably, curdling does occur, add another egg yolk: its addition will almost certainly produce the emulsification you have somehow earlier missed. When you have poured in oil twice to a total of ¼ cup, add approximately one fourth of the lemon juice and vinegar; at this point the emulsified mixture will begin to be stiff, but the addition of these acids will relax it. Continue to beat, adding oil and acids in these proportions until you have beaten in at least ¾ of a cup of oil, preferably the entire cup. Finish the sauce by adding 1 teaspoonful of salt, again superstitiously at the end. Adding the acids gradually, rather than as is sometimes advised after all the oil has been added, works quite as well and has one important advantage: if you put all the oil in first, you cannot tell how much acid you will need to relax the emulsified mixture to a proper consistency; it may be more acid than you want for flavor. Furthermore, the unrelaxed mixture will become so stiff that it will flake and fly from the beaters usually before you have worked in enough oil. By adding the acid gradually, you can control the consistency of the sauce throughout. The resulting mayonnaise will be less yellow, rather more shiny, than your being accustomed to bottled mayonnaises will lead you to expect. As you go on making mayonnaise you may well want to vary its seasoning; for example, I like more mustard, even as much as 1 tablespoonful.

Conversation piece: Very few seem to know the origin of the term *Mayonnaise*. The best account of it I have come on occurs in Nancy Mitford's *Madame de Pompadour*. In the first year of the Seven Years' War, the Maréchal de Richelieu, in command of the French fleet, set off to take the Island of Minorca, "of great importance as a vantage point for the English fleet. He had been besieging the supposedly impregnable Fort St. Philip, at Mahon, for a few weeks, and finding it a great bore in the absence of any women. His only pleasures were those of the table. But his cook was laboring under difficulties: there was no butter or cream on the island. He was driven to invent a new sauce, made only of eggs and oil, the Mahonnaise."

From Mayonnaise

Sauce Rémoulade: add to a cup of mayonnaise 2 tablespoonfuls of finely grated gherkins, 1 tablespoonful of capers (if you like them), 1 tablespoonful of chopped parsley and tarragon (the parsley alone will do if you haven't tarragon).

Tartar Sauce: (The classic version and not what ordinarily goes under the name.) Mash with a fork in a bowl the yolks of 2 hard-boiled eggs, and season them with salt and pepper; add 3 tablespoonfuls of oil and 1 of vinegar, and a finely grated small onion. Add enough mayonnaise to make a sauce of the proper consistency.

Green Sauce: boil briskly for two minutes in ¼ cup of water 1 tablespoonful each of chopped spinach, cress, parsley, and 1 teaspoonful of chopped tarragon. Pour off the water, wrap the greens in a small piece of cloth, and press to extract as much as you can of their rich green juice. Color and flavor with it a cup of mayonnaise.

4. SPECIAL DISHES

The "special" in this heading is used in a number of ways: in general, these are the dishes which give variety to meals like the meals of the thirty menus. It has been my lot to travel, often months on end. Happily, I have been able to eat, while traveling, in good hotels and good restaurants. Save in the very best restaurants, and probably even there, such fare eventually palls. The invariable remedy is to look for dishes that are in some way special.

The preceding thirty menus should minimize this need: each of them is intended to produce the dish in question at its best, as it could be produced only in a really great kitchen, where qualified cooks are available to devote themselves to the preparation of a meal for two special guests. But almost inevitably menu making becomes in some measure standard: a given meat, cooked in a given way; a suitable accompaniment; a salad; possibly a preliminary; possibly a dessert. Even such standard, and desirably standard, menus can be spiced by some difference.

"Special" in this heading means that spicing. It may be a standard meat, or fish, prepared in a different or unstandard way: it may even be a leftover meat or fish, which in its leftover form becomes more appetizing. It may be a standard or unstandard fish or meat accompanied by something also different. It may be even an unusually appetizing preliminary, or a salad or a dessert that is different. This is eating, *à la carte*, at its best.

A good beginning is with leftovers, least imaginably, for most, with leftover fish. To be sure, no fish should be left over long. For what are probably psychological reasons, almost any leftover fish has a rebirth (as Botticelli supposed Venus was born) in a scallop shell. Even small quantities of lobster or shrimp Américaine reappear happily in this form, particularly if enough of the sauce was left: pour it over the remaining meat in scallop shells, sprinkle with bread crumbs, dot with butter, and bake in a 350° oven till the crumbs are browned. Other fish reappears as happily if flaked into sauce *vin blanc* or sauce Mornay in the top of a double boiler over hot water, with the resulting mixture poured into shells, which are then briefly exposed to a preheated broiler to give the surface its characteristic flecks of brown. Even small quantities in this form make a fine preliminary for another meal, a taste of fish before something else.

Similarly small quantities of leftover meats lend themselves happily to what in French are called the *émincés*, not what is sometimes supposed to be the equivalent in English, *hash*. In a proper *émincé* the meat involved is not ground or chopped fine, but rather is cut in regular small slivers or even cubes. It is then warmed briefly (so that it will not toughen from further cooking) in an appropriate sauce, and is best served on slices of toast which convey the last drops of the sauce. This may be the remnants of its own sauce, as in the case of the Chicken Bercy of Menu 1 or the Veal Chasseur of Menu 26. It might well be sauce piquante or sauce Robert for leftover pork. Such meats somehow revive in such sauces and appeal to the eye, when, served on squares or rounds of toast, they are sprinkled with freshly chopped parsley, or better still, tarragon.

One leftover, mentioned in Menu 16, red-flannel hash, is for me an added reason for having a "boiled dinner." Its preparation is simple and the product can be near elegant.

Chop coarsely with the blade of your chef's knife the cold buttered vegetables left from the boiled dinner—carrots, beets, onions, potatoes, and cabbage. Grind finely in the meat grinder as much cold corned beef as you can spare. Put the ground meat and the chopped vegetables in a fry pan with no further grease than that which they contain and warm over low heat covered until they have yielded their grease. At this point, with your broad spatula, push the hash to half the fry pan's surface to make a thick crescent, and increase the heat to brown the bottom and side surfaces. As they begin to brown, work them loose from the pan's bottom and side with the spatula. When, with practice, you succeed in this procedure, you will achieve a fine brown crust that will hold firm when finally you turn the crescent out on the platter on which you serve it. To achieve it, sometimes it is well to add a little more grease (butter or vegetable fat) when the browning begins.

In the case of ham or tongue in sufficient quantities to be neatly sliced, a similar revival occurs in Sauce Madère. Indeed, with the slices warmed in this sauce, or particularly in the case of tongue, in sauce piquante, they really put in a fresh appearance.

Ordinarily beef does not submit well to such reheating, and in subsequent uses it is at its best simply in thin slices, cold, with salad. But if one tires of it cold, or wants it hot, there is one possibility that works well if the roast or steak is properly rare: a Beef paprika.

Cut leftover rare beef into ¾-inch squares, eliminating the browned crusty edges.

Fry a grated onion in 2 cubic inches of butter without browning, add the squares of beef, cover, and leave simmering.

Peel and deseed two or more tomatoes. When they are ready, add them to the onions and the meat and keep simmering for two hours, adding water if necessary.

Before serving, add 1 teaspoonful (or more) of paprika, ½ cup of sour cream, and salt to taste.

The traditional accompaniment of this dish is buttered noodles, i.e., egg noodles boiled for slightly less time than is indicated on the package, drained, reheated in a generous amount of butter, say 1 cubic inch, and served either as they are or with a crust of bread crumbs browned by reheating in the oven and brief exposure to the broiler.

One omnipresent leftover, mushroom stems, deserves special treatment in the kitchen and here, as the source of a most useful ingredient, always referred to in French cookery as *duxelles*. It is quickly prepared, keeps well in the refrigerator, and seen there suggests a variety of uses.

Finely chop 2 shallots or grate half an onion, and fry with a clove of garlic in 1 cubic inch of butter, not letting either onion or garlic brown.

Wash and chop coarsely the mushroom stems with your long knife.

Fry them gently with the onion and garlic till they cease to steam, or about ten minutes. Salt and pepper. Remove the garlic.

Chop and add 2 tablespoonfuls of parsley.

Finish by adding ¼ cup of white wine and cooking further till the liquid has disappeared and the mixture is again buttery.

Refrigerate in a closed jar: it will keep well in proper cold for at least a week.

This mixture was called for in the Stuffed Tomatoes of Menu 15. It has many other uses, as, for example, with the cottage cheese stuffing for the Stuffed Pancakes of Menu 20, as a variant to the stuffing there suggested; it provides an engaging variant to the bread stuffing for small roast birds; it gives a special zest to a mushroom omelet.

Conversation piece: I cherish the hope that the inclusion of *Duxelles* in this book will lead some scholarly reader to explain its origin. Such research as I have undertaken toward this end has led me no further than to Nicolas du Blé, Marquis d'Uxelles, who defended and surrendered Mainz during the War of the Grand Alliance under Louis XIV. The eponymous heroes of *haute cuisine*, however, are usually connected with what is named for them by a fondness for its ingredients; and I have yet to find any connection between the marquis and mushrooms.

Speaking of omelets, they and eggs in other forms should figure more among "special dishes" than is usual in the United States. Except for those who can't eat eggs for various reasons they often tempt the appetite more even at dinner or at a late supper than any other dish on the bill of fare, and more than ever when made tempting in some special way. For most Americans, the range of omelets, for example, is ordinarily limited to three or four, with cheese, mushrooms, ham, and sometimes "*fines herbes*" which usually turn out to be one herb, parsley; the true *omelette aux fines herbes* calls for four: parsley, chervil, tarragon, and chives; lacking the last three, an omelet in this style will certainly be better if even some dried marjoram, for example, is mixed in with parsley.

Here is the recommended procedure for omelet making referred to in Part I:

In a mixing bowl make a basic mixture of as many eggs (and I recommend not attempting an omelet made of more than four) as you want, 1 teaspoonful of sour cream, 1/4 teaspoonful of salt, and five grinds of the pepper grinder for each egg. Melt 1 cubic inch of butter in a frying pan over low heat, and while it is melting beat the egg mixture well but not to full frothiness. Increasing the heat under the frying pan to near its top, pour in the beaten mixture; as it begins to solidify, keep it floating on the butter by moving the pan back and forth with your left hand on its handle; with a spatula in your right hand begin "scrambling" the mixture, by drawing back from the edge what has begun to solidify there, tilting the pan with your left hand to allow to flow there still liquid mixture from the top. Repeat this process around the pan's edge till there is no more liquid to flow, though some will remain on the top of the "scrambled eggs" that have been accumulating toward the pan's center. During this process reduce and heighten the heat on the omelet by lifting it from the heat as you work, less heat as you scramble, more as you allow liquid to flow to the edge. When only a little liquid remains on the top, remove the pan to the kitchen shelf, and there, with the spatula, fold the omelet back once on itself into a half-moon shape, with the straight side parallel to the handle of the pan. So placed, you can turn it readily onto a warmed serving platter to be served as it is, plain; before you fold it you can place along the line on which you will fold it such garnishings as follow. If you prefer your omelet brown, you can turn it into a heat-resistant dish and brown it as you will under a preheated broiler—if it is a cheese omelet, with some of the cheese on top. Sometimes, if the added ingredients are small, as in the case of chopped herbs or duxelles, they are better added to the beaten egg mixture.

There follow a few of the other types of omelets that are classic in French cookery (some twenty-five in *L'Art Culinaire Français*):

Omelette Grand'mère: fry ¼-inch squares of white bread in butter till they are crisp and brown; lay half of them along the axis of the fold, and scatter the rest over the finished product.

Asparagus Omelet: really a plain omelet garnished with cooked asparagus tips lightly fried in butter; arrange them in little bouquets at the ends and sides of the omelet on its platter.

Omelette Rossini: have ready *pâté de foie gras*, part in little cubes, part in larger slices. Fold in the little cubes along the axis of the omelet, and lay the slices on its top; they will heat sufficiently in brief exposure to the broiler flame.

Conversation piece: The name Rossini (the composer) offers a fine example of the eponymous hero of *haute cuisine:* he was noted for his addiction to *pâté de foie gras*, and any dish that bears his name contains it.

Few Americans are aware of any range of "dropped," or more properly poached, eggs beyond the simple breakfast variety on toast, or possibly what has come to be known in the United States as Eggs Benedict: poached eggs on a thin slice of ham, laid in turn on a toasted English muffin, with the eggs covered with Hollandaise Sauce. An engaging variation I have recently encountered is known as Eggs Balch: eggs similarly served on English muffins, with the ham replaced by a slice of smoked salmon and the Hollandaise replaced by Sauce Béarnaise. On the other hand, *L'Art Culinaire* offers poached eggs in thirty-five varieties. Essentially, these are poached eggs, served on rounds of toast, with different sauces. The ways that follow will suggest others, as you have small quantities of sauces left over:

Poached Eggs Grand Duke: fry in butter rounds of bread (such as you can readily cut out with a cookie cutter or a can top); lay poached eggs on them in a heat-resistant platter, and pour over each egg Sauce Mornay; brown under the broiler. The full recipe calls for a shrimp and a slice of truffle under each egg; but they're good enough without this embellishment.

Poached Eggs Normande: lay poached eggs on rounds of toast and cover with Sauce Normande; in the full recipe poached oysters are served in the sauce.

Poached Eggs Chasseur: lay poached eggs on rounds of toast and cover with Sauce Chasseur, such as you may have left from Menu 10; if any of the veal was left, you could cut it finely and spread it under the egg on the toast.

In other styles the toast is replaced with vegetables, for example, artichoke bottoms such as can now be bought in cans or jars.

Poached Eggs Beaugency: lay poached eggs on artichoke bottoms and cover them with Sauce Béarnaise.

One other such style, which appears occasionally on American menus, is worth noting.

Poached Eggs Florentine: on boiled and buttered spinach lay dropped eggs in a heat-resistant platter; cover completely with Sauce Mornay, and sprinkle on it grated cheese and bread crumbs dotted with butter; brown under the broiler.

One should not forget the possibilities of so-called shirred eggs. As earlier remarked, they are better described, when properly cooked, by their French name, *oeufs au miroir;* broken gently into just-melted butter in an oven dish, and baked slowly in a 200° oven, their tender whites should be mirror bright. They do not figure in French cookery in the variety of poached eggs, but they offer engaging possibilities for experimentation. For example, they strongly appealed to me for luncheon on the day this was written, because of the presence in the refrigerator of some leftover Sauce Amandine of Menu 3 (almond slivers browned in brown butter). With some of it sprinkled around their edges, and with the further addition of four of the little Vienna sausages that come in cans, they provided a most congenial luncheon dish.

Likewise not to be forgotten, particularly when the appetite is delicate, are baked eggs, *oeufs en cocotte:* eggs gently dropped into a little butter melted in a custard cup, salted, peppered, and topped with 1 tablespoonful of cream, slowly baked in a 200° oven in a baking pan of water still further to slow their cooking.

Another special dish, mainly of eggs, is included here for readers able to make and handle piecrust:

Quiche Lorraine: line a low-sided pie plate with pastry as you would for any pie. Slice 5 long strips of bacon crosswise into ½-inch squares and fry till brown and crisp; drain on a paper towel. Slice in similar thin ½-inch squares about the same quantity of Swiss cheese. Spread first the bacon, and then on it the cheese, on the pastry. Beat 6 eggs first alone and then with ½ pint of cream and 1 teaspoonful of salt; pour over the bacon and the cheese, and dot the top with butter. Bake in a 400° oven till firm and brown on top. A Quiche in these proportions obviously will provide the main course of a luncheon for four or five persons.

A special delicacy involving eggs is to be thought of, both for itself and in case the moment ever comes when you decide for once to splurge on truffles: it is recommended by their purveyors as one of the best ways of enjoying them. Actually it is the Italian version of the sturdier Swiss Fondue of Menu 20.

Fonduta: the recommended cheese is Italian Fontina, but it is very like Swiss cheese and the latter serves almost as well. Cut enough cheese into ¼-inch cubes to produce 1 cupful. Put them cold into ½ cup of milk in a frying pan. Have ready the beaten yolk of 1 egg diluted with 1 tablespoonful of milk. Slowly heat the milk, constantly stirring the cheese cubes. When they have melted, add the beaten egg yolk to the paste and serve, when its thickening is complete, on rounds or slices of toast. If truffles are to be included, they are simply sliced and spread over the top.

Two other Italian dishes figure at this point, where one traditionally finds *pasta* on the bill of fare.

Gnocchi, Roman style: in a thick-bottomed saucepan bring to a boil 1 quart of milk to which have been added 2 cubic inches of butter, 1 teaspoonful of salt, and a little grated nutmeg. Into the boiling milk stir a paste of ¾ cup of coarse corn meal, white or yellow, mixed with ½ cup of cold water, to prevent lumping. Stir frequently. After it has cooked for at least ten minutes, to the consistency of breakfast cereal, add ½ cup of grated spaghetti cheese. When the cheese has melted into the corn-meal mush, remove the mixture from the stove, and, after cooling slightly, add to it 1 beaten egg. Spread in a buttered baking dish and refrigerate. When it is thoroughly chilled, cut it in squares, or, preferably, rounds, lifting each square or round out with a spatula. Dip each of them in melted butter and then in coarsely grated Swiss cheese. Bake in a 400° oven for fifteen minutes, or until brown. The gnocchi may be eaten by themselves or with a spaghetti sauce. (As in Menu 3, it is economical in time and butter to melt the butter and dip the pieces in it in the same dish in which they are to be baked.)

The last of these three Italian dishes, unlike the delicate Fonduta, is a sturdy dish, and has for me served a variety of purposes, principally as a main dish, outdoors in Maine, at supper parties in New York, and is even better, almost, when warmed over, as a refrigerator stand-by. It is, of course, an Italian version, with characteristic alterations, of the Middle Eastern pilaf of Menu 8. These proportions yield enough for four.

Risotto: chop or crush into small pieces dried mushrooms (such as you can buy at any Italian grocery) to yield approximately a ¼ cup; bring them to a boil in 1 cup of water, and leave them soaking.

In a saucepan that will go into the oven fry brown in 2 cubic inches of butter 2 tablespoonfuls (or more) of *pignolias* (pine nuts, likewise procurable in Italian groceries). Lift them out with a perforated spoon; crush them with a pestle or with your thumb in the bowl of a teaspoon, and keep them for later use.

In the same butter fry without browning 1 clove of garlic and 1 grated onion.

Cut into small cubes whatever leftover meat you have: chicken, lamb, pork, or, best, ham. Remove the garlic and fry with the onion.

Add 2 cups of rice, and stir till it is thoroughly impregnated with the greasy mixture in the pan.

Add 4 cups of water, or meat broth if you have any, the mushrooms and their broth, ¼ cup of raisins, and bring to a boil.

Then add the crushed pine nuts, stirring them in, and 1 tablespoonful of chopped parsley.

Put the mixture in a 350° oven and cook for thirty minutes. It should by then, when stirred with a fork, produce rice in separate grains, shiny with the rich sauce, slightly chewy, or *al dente*, as the Italians say.

Risotto is served with grated spaghetti cheese and red wine.

These sea-food specialties demand inclusion. The first is seasonal, when shad are running.

Shad Roe: pour ¼ cup of melted butter onto a square of aluminum foil and rub in it the shad roes; wrap them so that the roes are hermetically sealed and bake them sealed for twenty minutes in a 350° oven. Serve in their butter. As noted, Sauce Mousseline goes remarkably well with the roes, and with asparagus, which is in season at much the same time.

The second sea-food dish is quite as practicable to cook in the United States as it is to eat in France—mussels, although you may have to look for them in the main fish markets, or in Italian fish shops. Among the ways of cooking them, two seem particularly rewarding, one merely an extension of the other.

Mussels Marinière: scrub each mussel with a stiff vegetable brush under running water and put each to wash further in a soup kettle of cold water: watch to see if any is suspiciously heavy; occasionally an otherwise innocent shell is filled with mud, and one such will not improve the finished dish; eliminate any that are suspicious. Do not leave them long in water, as it opens the shells and deprives them of their juice. As soon as the scrubbing is completed, remove them from the water, and pour it off. Replace them in the kettle and scatter over them ten grinds from the pepper grinder, 3 tablespoonfuls of chopped shallots or grated onion, a little thyme, and 1 cup of white wine. Cook, covered, for ten minutes over a medium flame, or until they all have opened. Pour the broth that will have formed in good quantity into a saucepan, leaving the mussels to keep warm in the kettle. Briskly boil the broth to reduce it by half, adding to it 2 cubic inches of butter and at the last minute 1 tablespoonful of chopped parsley. Serve the mussels in soup plates in their shells, with the resulting sauce poured over them.

Mussels Poulette: before starting to cook the mussels as above, prepare in the top of a double boiler by cooking it fifteen minutes a white *roux* of 2 cubic inches of butter and 2 tablespoonfuls of flour. When the broth of the mussels is ready, pour it into this *roux*, and cook to make what is essentially a velvet. Finish it with ¼ cup of cream and thicken it finally with 2 beaten egg yolks diluted with 1 tablespoonful of cream, again adding chopped parsley at the last moment.

The third sea-food specialty is an unusually fine way of cooking a New England stand-by, finnan haddie, smoked filets of haddock.

With a fork knead into 1 cubic inch of butter 1 tablespoonful of arrowroot flour. Put a piece of finnan haddie (I prefer a thick slice from the center of the filet, 1 pound for two persons) in a frying pan, pour over it 1 pint of milk, and add one onion in ½-inch slices, broken into rings, five grinds on the pepper grinder, ⅛ teaspoonful of thyme, ⅛ teaspoonful of marjoram, and the butter and arrowroot flour. Simmer over gentle heat till the arrowroot flour has thickened the milk. Butter a baking dish, and transfer to it the finnan haddie, pouring over it the now creamy sauce. Dot its surface with 1 cubic inch of butter and bake in a 350° oven till its top begins to brown. Serve in its baking dish.

It may seem strange that meats do not figure in this à la carte section, as they would, traditionally, at this point in a bill of fare. There are, of course, numerous "special" ways of serving them, some of which have already been dealt with in their "leftover" uses, others which call for them in sauces in such special containers as the fluffy French pastry cups known as *vols au vent*, and others still which require special procedures, like the making of croquettes, which will be dealt with below in Section 9. But meats in general are best treated in the more or less standard ways indicated in the thirty menus, and accordingly this bill of fare moves to special ways of cooking vegetables.

A vegetable platter: in most shops now it is possible to find in small tins tiny carrots, beets, onions, and even small, well-rounded potatoes. Every so often it is a treat to utilize these beautifully prepared vegetables, neatly arranged in rows across a platter or dish in which you can simply heat them in melted butter in the oven. They are made more attractive still by a light sprinkling of chopped parsley at the last moment.

Flemish Carrots: scrape and slice small, tender carrots lengthwise into strips approximately ¼-inch square and 3 to 4 inches long. Cook them covered in a heavy aluminum saucepan in 1 cubic inch of butter for twenty minutes over a gentle flame, stirring them occasionally. Finish with ¼ cup of sweet or sour cream and 1 tablespoonful of chopped parsley.

Potatoes Anna: salt and pepper ¼ cup of melted butter and mix it well into as many ⅛-inch slices as 2 medium potatoes will yield. (Again you can do this economically in time and butter by melting the butter in the dish in which the potatoes are to bake—best, in this instance, a metal pie plate to which you can fit some cover.) Arrange the buttered slices in layers flat on the pan, with the smaller slices slanted at the edges. Cover, and bake for an hour in a 350° oven. When finished, those on the bottom and the edges should be well browned and crusty. If toward the time you want them they are not browned, uncover and increase the oven heat. If you can manage it, and with practice you will, Potatoes Anna should be tipped out upside down to serve, with the fine brown of the bottom and edges well displayed.

Cauliflower or Broccoli Mornay: cook broccoli by steaming hardly more than ten minutes, so that it remains bright green; cauliflower by boiling in ample water, fifteen minutes. Arrange the pieces in a heat-resistant dish, keeping warm if necessary in a slow oven. Pour over Sauce Mornay and finish under the broiler with the briefest exposure necessary to give the sauce its characteristic touches of brown.

Radishes in Béchamel: rarely served as a cooked vegetable, red radishes turn out to be a distinct addition when, with the tops and roots removed, they are boiled in salted water for fifteen minutes, drained, and served in white sauce.

Jerusalem Artichokes: not true artichokes, but rather the tubers of a sunflower, this vegetable may be served simply boiled, whole like boiled potatoes in melted butter, or puréed through the Foley Food Mill like mashed potatoes. There is no need to peel their knobby surfaces: their skin is delicate, and they are sufficiently prepared for cooking simply by scrubbing them hard with a vegetable brush.

Mashed Sweet Potatoes: boil sweet potatoes thirty minutes in their skins; drain, and cool. When they are cool, their skins will peel off readily with a vegetable knife. Slice them crosswise into ½-inch slices and purée them through the Foley Food Mill. Add 1 cubic inch of butter, ½ teaspoonful of salt, ten grinds on the pepper grinder, and ¼ cup of marsala (or sherry). Turn the purée into a cocotte and warm it for five minutes in a 300° oven.

Purée of Celery Root: pare 2 knobs and slice into ½-inch slices. Boil them for an hour in half water and half beef consommé till the liquid has almost disappeared. Purée the slices through the Foley Food Mill, and put the purée in the top of a double boiler to keep warm and to reduce if it is too thin. Finish by adding ¼ cup of sour cream and 1 cubic inch of butter.

Purée of Chestnuts: one of the greatest vegetables, but frankly troublesome to prepare *until* you get the hang of it. It pays to pay a bit more for the chestnuts you buy in order to minimize the trouble of opening them by getting the larger nuts. Lay each nut on its flat side and on the rounding side incise a ¾ inch cross with the point of a sharp knife: the incision should be deep enough to penetrate both the outer and inner skins. Bring a saucepan of water to a boil and immerse in it not more than 20 of the chestnuts for five minutes at a time. Removing no more than 5 at once, you should, with a vegetable knife, be able to peel off both the outer shell and the inner skin. The optimum time for doing so is just after about five minutes' boiling, and you should be able to peel the first 20 within the optimum period. With two pans of boiling water you can keep the process continuous. While you're at it, it's well to peel at least 2 pounds, since there is a variety of uses for the purée. (See p. 190, "Desserts.") With this variety of uses in view, begin by simply making an unflavored purée of the nuts that came through peeling somewhat damaged or in fragments, as some may. Set aside the perfect specimens. Make the purée by boiling in a quart of water about an hour, or until most of the nuts have more or less puréed themselves, and finish by passing the mixture through the Foley Food Mill. To finish as a vegetable, simply add ¼ cup of cream, 1 cubic inch of butter, and 1 teaspoonful of salt. This purée is the traditional accompaniment of all kinds of game, turkey, goose, and even beefsteak.

Brussels Sprouts and Chestnuts: the most desirable Brussels sprouts are the smallest; if they are to be found only in the larger sizes, the waste involved in drastically removing the outer leaves is made up for by the improvement in quality. Cook the peeled sprouts by steaming not more than ten minutes, so that they remain bright green. Five minutes before serving, melt 1 cubic inch of butter in a frying pan and lightly fry the sprouts together with as many whole chestnuts as you are prepared to invest in the dish.

Mushrooms: this vegetable figured in the thirty menus only as an ingredient, save in the Morning Mushrooms of Menu 6. Three ways of preparing them as a separate vegetable follow.

(1) Remove the stems and wash as many mushrooms as you wish to serve. Fry them slowly in 1 cubic inch of butter first with their hollow sides down; turn them over, and salt and pepper each on the hollow side; cook for three minutes more. In this cooking the salt will bring their brown juice into the hollows at the same time as the caps brown slightly. Finish by turning over the heads again, quickly deglazing the pan with this juice. If you wish, you can finish the dish with the juice of half a lemon.

(2) Proceed as with (1) till the final stage, when removing the caps to their serving dish, and keeping them warm, you finally deglaze the pan with a little sherry and make a sauce by adding ¼ cup of sour cream. Pour this sauce on the heads and serve.

(3) Proceed as with (1) till the final stage, when, removing the caps,

fill the hollow of each with as much Duxelles as it will hold; arrange the heads in a buttered baking dish, hollow side down, pour over them the sauce from the pan, sprinkle with grated spaghetti cheese, and bake in a 350° oven for five minutes.

Zucchini (the elongated, green, summer squash that usually goes by this name): buy the smallest you can find, and scrub them well under running water with a vegetable brush; minute quantities of fine dirt tend to cling to their slightly sticky surfaces. Cut the zucchinis crosswise into ¼-inch slices. Fry them lightly in 1 cubic inch of butter in a frying pan with a cover, turning them over and over till each slice is gilded with the butter, but not letting them brown. Season with 1 teaspoonful of salt, five grinds on the pepper grinder, and five grates on the nutmeg grater. Add ½ cup of water, cover, and let simmer for five minutes over low heat. Just before serving, remove the cover and cook over moderate heat till the water has cooked away and the slices are covered with the again buttery sauce. If you prefer, you may allow them to brown a bit at this point, or serve them, as I prefer them, with the flesh golden, and framed in the still bright green of the skin.

5. SALADS

A la carte, the most constructive approach to salads is via their dressings: first, the oil, or French, dressings and their derivatives; second, mayonnaise and its derivatives.

The basis of all the *oil dressings* is much the same: rub the bowl, whenever possible the bowl in which the salad is to be made, with a crushed clove of garlic; even the toughest clove will crush under the pressure of two thumbs; I crush it into small pieces and rub the bowl hard, then remove the pieces. For salad for two, add ½ teaspoonful of salt, five grinds on the pepper grinder, and 1 tablespoonful of vinegar; stir this mixture till the salt is dissolved, and then add 2 or 3 tablespoonfuls of olive oil, as you prefer. Just before serving, beat vigorously with a spoon to emulsify the oil and vinegar into a whitish, creamy sauce.

Minor variations on this basic dressing follow:

Add ½ teaspoonful of mustard, dry or prepared, to the salt and pepper before dissolving the salt in vinegar.

Vary the vinegars, e.g., red wine vinegar, white wine vinegar, malt vinegar, or through the various vinegars flavored with herbs, most notably tarragon and dill.

Flavor the salad with chopped fresh herbs: I say the salad rather than the dressing, because if the herbs are added to the dressing before the last minute the vinegar will turn them from their bright green to brown; this is most readily avoided by sprinkling them on the salad greens.

As this implies, the basic dressings are at their best in what are ordinarily called the green salads. Some of them, however, almost indicate the dressing to be used. Fine Bibb lettuce, now becoming available in better vegetable shops, has so fine a flavor and succulence of its own as to call for only the basic dressing. Water cress, as Virgil Thomson points out, has a spiciness that allows, even urges, omitting vinegar and using little if any pepper. Most green-salad makers tend to forget the full range of ingredients; thus the following check list is useful for reference:

Native or Boston lettuce: the inner portions only in its small separate leaves.

Hearts of this same lettuce: cut lengthwise in quarters.

Romaine: the inner portions only in its separate leaves.

Romaine hearts: again cut lengthwise in quarters.

Chicory: only the tenderer inner leaves; to reach them readily, trim off the tops and outer leaves drastically with your big knife.

Endive: peel off any discolored outer leaves; endive may be served in inch-long crosswise slices, broken out into separate leaves, though true amateurs of this salad prefer the stalks cut lengthwise into quarters.

Escarolle: as in the case of chicory, only the tenderer inner leaves, most readily reached by drastic trimming with the big knife. (Incidentally, this is the same green as endive, but is grown above ground, whereas endive is the usually later winter growth from its root, grown banked with earth.)

Water cress: the leaves and upper stems only; most readily prepared by cutting off the tough stems while the bunch is still intact.

Field salad (the French *mâche*): now becoming available in the autumn and winter in better vegetable shops; the roots of each small plant should be cut off, and the leaves should be thoroughly washed, best in a pot of water in which any clinging dirt can sink.

Occasionally to be added to green salads for variety are:

Celery: ⅛-inch crosswise slices.

Celery root: in the 2-inch long, ¼-inch square slivers, known as *juliennes.*

Radishes: the red or white in ⅛-inch crosswise slices; the black, strong variety, in *juliennes,* and only for the sturdy.

Tomatoes: preferably not regular tomatoes, since sliced, or even quartered, their juice tends to be a dilutant of the dressing, but rather the small varieties, red or yellow plum tomatoes, or red or yellow cherry tomatoes that come into the market in the fall and can be washed and served whole with greens.

Many, it seems to me, go to unnecessary pains in washing and particularly in drying salad greens. When well washed in running water, or from soaking in water in a pot, they can be sufficiently dried for all practical purposes by allowing them to remain for half an hour in paper towels, turning them occasionally so that any surplus moisture runs off into the towels. If the towels become too wet to absorb more moisture, change them. In serving, when the dressing has been emulsified by beating, greens so prepared are simply placed in the salad bowl and stirred until each leaf is well covered with the dressing: the French prefer them labored, i.e., stirred till they are limp; most Americans prefer less stirring to conserve their natural crispness.

One other salad ingredient deserves special mention—alligator pears or avocados. Their delicate flavor is at its best with no more than the simplest oil dressing. They seem to me best enjoyed simply cut in half and served with the stone removed, the center filled with oil dressing, to be eaten with a dessert spoon. They can equally well be cut in half and peeled, sliced crosswise, and included in a green salad, or served on a platter in slices. In any case, they should be opened or peeled only just before serving, as they tend to turn brown with exposure to the air. Your fruit man will probably do better than you in selecting one at the precise point of ripeness for it to be at its best. I often buy several hard, unripe ones, and keep them till ripe for eating: they then yield slightly to finger pressure.

Two dressings derived from the basic oil dressing deserve special note.

The first is Sauce Vinaigrette: to the basic sauce of salt, pepper, vinegar, and oil add 1 tablespoonful of finely chopped shallots or finely grated onion, and, at the last minute, 1 tablespoonful of chopped herbs—at least parsley, and if possible tarragon, chervil, or possibly chives. For decoration, sprinkle more of these chopped herbs over the salad before serving.

Sauce Vinaigrette is at its best on vegetables, of which again a check list follows:

Tomatoes: thinly sliced, preferably with their skins on to keep their shape. Arrange in rows.

Asparagus: best when steamed only just long enough before serving to cool in time; otherwise, it tends to be watery: in that case, it should be thoroughly dried before using.

Artichokes: as in Menu 20, or in the form of artichoke bottoms, arranged on a platter.

String beans: leftover beans can perfectly well be used in this form.

Green cabbage: with this sauce finely shredded cabbage yields a particularly fine coleslaw.

Cucumbers: but preferably with the special treatment noted, i.e., salting on a platter half an hour in advance to extract their water, which can then be poured off, to avoid its diluting the sauce. They will lose their crispness, but true amateurs prefer them limp, and others who cannot eat them ordinarily find them quite digestible in this form.

The second dressing derived from the basic sauce is

Lorenzo Dressing: oil dressing to which is added 1 tablespoonful of tomato ketchup, and at the last minute to conserve their greenness, ½ cup of chopped water cress leaves.

In my experience of it, Lorenzo Dressing seems to demand one green, and one only—romaine, and preferably the quartered inner leaves.

For salads with mayonnaise, the same ingredients serve as for those with Sauce Vinaigrette. Well arranged on a platter (with the exception of string beans and cabbage), they are usually served with a narrow strip of mayonnaise on them, and more offered in a bowl. Such blander salads seem called for with more delicate cold meats and aspics. They are particularly happy in a cold buffet, both for their flavor and for their appearance.

Happier still, for both reasons, on such an occasion are what the French call *salades composées;* one generally known in the United States is the so-called Waldorf Salad of celery, apple, and walnuts. One such has appeared in Menu 24; another, classic in that it is derived from Escoffier, will serve as an example and suggest others.

Salade Beaucaire: at least an hour in advance of serving make an oil dressing seasoned only with mustard (omitting the salt and pepper from the vinegar and oil) and set to soak in it ⅛-inch crosswise slices of celery, endive, and 2-inch long ¼-inch square slivers of celery root in approximately equal quantities. An hour later add to this mixture thin slivers of cooked ham, again 2 inches long and ¼-inch square, ⅛-inch lengthwise slices of tart apples, and ⅛-inch slices across the heads of well-washed raw mushrooms, again in approximately equal quantities. Bind this mixture with mayonnaise and transfer it to the bowl in which it is to be served. On the top, around the edge of the bowl, arrange cooked beet slices (slices of canned beets serve perfectly well, but dry them on a paper towel so that none of their juice remains to stain the other ingredients). Sprinkle the top, the beets included, with finely chopped parsley and, if possible, tarragon, and mound a little pile of the herbs in the center for decoration. Serve with more mayonnaise in a bowl.

Similar salads, like the Belle Hortense of Menu 24, utilize mayonnaise in its derived forms, particularly Sauce Rémoulade.

Not properly salads, but logically included here, are other uses of mayonnaise and its derived sauces, particularly Sauce Rémoulade and Green Mayonnaise, such as their use with sea foods, e.g., lobsters, crab, and shrimp. The appeal of such dishes likewise depends in some measure on their presentation: for example, Crab Rémoulade, prepared simply by blending (gently in order not to fragment the tender pieces) crab meat and the sauce, is well presented in individual scallop shells, with a sprinkling of chopped herbs, and, if you are patient enough, a border of yellow egg yolks pulverized by pressing them through a sieve.

6. ASPICS

The United States has long been a country of gelatin desserts, particularly since it became possible to prepare them from flavored crystalline gelatin in an envelope. In recent years it has neglected another and, to me, more interesting type of jelly, known generically as *aspic*—meat jelly. It figured earlier even in home cookery, for in literature the classic gesture toward invalids was to take them meat jelly, as something easy to eat and most nourishing.

Its recent neglect is undoubtedly because of the seeming difficulty of preparing it. Its basis is always some meat stock, usually beef or veal, together with the bones, which is made still more gelatinous by the addition of calves' feet. As I have twice remarked, the making of such a stock requires at least eight hours' simmering, and a finally inevitably messy clarification with egg whites. With the meats involved now as expensive as they are, and with no coal or wood stove on which simmering can be an easy by-product of other cooking and of heating the kitchen, making a stock for yourself is inevitably costly. Finally, calves' feet are not always readily found, even in a market district. In the belief that an aspic stock prepared in the classic manner must be superior, I have made it any number of times, and rather enjoyed its making, only to come to the final conclusion that it was not sufficiently, if at all, superior to the aspic I could produce by a procedure hardly more complicated than making a dessert from prepared, flavored gelatin.

This procedure has been given in the context of preparing individual aspics of *pâté de foie gras* in Menu 24; but, for convenience, it will be repeated here in more generalized terms. Its simple secret is, again, using canned stock—consommé:

Put to soften in ¼ cup of white wine 1 teaspoonful of unflavored crystalline gelatin. If you are to use your aspic in molds, it is well at this point to start them chilling in the refrigerator, best in its freezing unit.

When the gelatin in the wine has softened to form a paste, pour a 10½-ounce can of beef consommé "with gelatin added" into the top of a double boiler, and over moderate direct heat stir into it the pasty gelatin, continuing to heat only till the gelatin is thoroughly dissolved. While it is dissolving, fill the double boiler bottom with ice cubes, and when it is dissolved put the double boiler top on them. Stirring occasionally, let the mixture cool. Note that when cool, over the ice, it will more quickly than you think turn first syrupy, and then too solid to handle well; in general it is best handled when cool but not syrupy. While it is cooling add ¼ cup of marsala or sherry. If it becomes syrupy, remove the double boiler top immediately from the ice, or even stop the process by setting it briefly in warm water: happily, this jellying is an easily reversible process.

If, as is frequently the case, you are using aspic as a decorative coating sauce for some heavy ingredient such as *pâté de foie gras,* as soon as it is cool, fill your mold or molds, chilled from the refrigerator, half full of liquid aspic and return them to the refrigerator to jell—not to the freezing unit where the aspic will quickly freeze.

While the aspic in the half-filled molds is jellying, prepare whatever it is to surround. If it is a *pâté* for individual aspics, as in Menu 24, shape it into small rounds or squares, most conveniently on a piece of aluminum foil, using the blade of a table knife, and remembering that clean fingers are sometimes the best tool in the kitchen. Or if you plan to use one larger mold, and consequently want your *pâté* in one larger appropriately shaped piece, model it on the foil much as you would model in clay; for my larger mold, the *pâté* extracted whole from two oval cans, rounded off on the top with the excess modeled in at the base, produces a solid piece much the same shape as my mold.

When the aspic in the half-filled molds is firm, not necessarily hard, place on it the *pâté:* the small pieces for individual molds can simply be picked up in your fingers or on a knife blade; the larger piece for the larger mold can easily be placed by putting your right hand under the foil, holding it, and guiding it into position with your left hand as you invert it into the mold with your right hand. When it is well placed in the center of the firm aspic, with an equal space between it and the sides of the mold, pour in the rest of the aspic from the double boiler top; there is no harm if at this point it is syrupy. As noted in Menu 24, it is a nice touch to paint the *pâté* once or more with liquid aspic on a butter brush to assure that the aspic poured in last will adhere to its otherwise greasy surface; but this step is not essential.

Always prepare aspics well in advance, long enough so that they may be entirely firm at least an hour before you intend to use them. An hour before use, remove them from their mold or molds by the following procedure: fill a pan large enough for the purpose with water as hot as it comes from the faucet; hold the mold by its edges and dip it into the hot water until the aspic in it begins to move as you tip it slightly. If you are dealing with individual molds, you can turn their contents with a quick flip on to the platter on which you intend to serve them; if with a larger mold, invert the platter over its bottom, and turn the platter back to normal position, holding the mold tightly to it in proper position in its center with your right hand. If smaller molds fail on first try to yield their contents, you will find that you can give them another dip and another flip. If the larger mold fails to yield, you can persuade it to either by covering it with a dish towel wrung out in hot water laid closely over it, or simply by letting it sit a bit till room temperature proves persuasive.

Don't be concerned if some of the outer aspic in this process runs on the platter. Refrigerate it again to let the aspics firm up again and to have the platter chilled for service. Just before serving, you can scrape, with a spoon, any aspic that did run into small regularly placed sparkling piles as a decoration.

At this point you will be glad to have made more aspic than your molds required. If you did, pour it into some flat dish, e.g., an oven dish, so that it is not more than ¾ inch thick, and refrigerate when you refrigerate your molds. When you have removed the aspic from the molds, remove this aspic from its dish by the same warming procedure, inverting the dish on a piece of aluminum foil. On the foil, cut it into cubes or diamonds, and place them evenly on the platter's edge as a decoration. Or smaller quantities can simply be scraped from the dish and chopped with a spoon to augment what ran from the aspics when they were first turned out. Another decorative possibility is to force this spooned-out surplus through one of the corrugated spouts of a pastry bag or a cake decorator of the syringe type in various decorative patterns. When you learn to handle it, decoratively, aspic is the cook's delight.

If you are serving aspic in hot weather, as you often will, it is well to serve it over ice. A round silver platter on which I often serve aspic from individual molds fits exactly over a large shallow glass bowl otherwise used to float flowers in: filled with ice cubes, it keeps aspics firm in the hottest weather.

As the foregoing implies, aspic, in classic cookery, serves three functions: first, it keeps some choice and moist ingredient choice and moist; second, it serves as its flavorable sauce; third, as the cook's delight, it opens up a wide variety of decorative possibilities. These three functions will be illustrated here by only a few of its other uses.

Eggs in aspic: as remarked earlier, this is a favorite French *hors d'oeuvre.* Poach as many eggs as you wish to serve in water held just under a boil and acidulated by a few drops of vinegar. Poach them till they are perhaps a little firmer than you would want them for hot dishes, i.e., till their yolks bleed only from the center when they are cut. Trim off any of the outer spreading white and let them cool in cold water. Fill half full with aspic some mold large enough to encompass the eggs and refrigerate to allow it to firm: my custard cups serve this purpose well; teacups would do. When this aspic is firm, with your fingers lay the poached egg on it, sunny side down, so that the yolk will be up when you serve it, and fill the molds with the remaining aspic. Traditionally, the aspic for this dish is flavored slightly with tarragon (you easily can flavor it with a teaspoonful of tarragon vinegar) and is decorated with a sprig of tarragon leaves in the firm jelly before the eggs are laid on it; traditionally, too, it is finished with a thin slice of ham cut to the shape of the mold and laid on the egg before the final aspic is poured in. But these additions are not essential. Serve the aspics turned out of their molds on a platter, returned to the refrigerator to firm them and to chill well before serving, and, if you wish, decorated as above.

Molded aspics need not be restricted to the various pastes, *pâté de foie gras,* and its humbler but excellent relatives, such as the pastes of lesser livers, ham, and chicken that are now made in the United States. For example, surprisingly, cold lobster and even shrimp find this meat jelly congenial. If such solid ingredients are used, a large aspic cannot be served by slicing across it with a reasonably sharp knife. Rather, it is served with a spoon, with which the solid pieces come along with their share of the aspic as their sauce.

One classic variant on this basic procedure merits inclusion, particularly since many people enjoy it—mousse of ham:

Mousse of ham: prepare the basic aspic. Instead of pouring half of it into the chilled mold (in this case preferably a single larger mold) merely pour in enough to coat lightly the inside of the mold with it, as you can by rocking and rotating the little in the mold; only the thinnest coating is needed, for its function here is not that of a decorative coating but rather only as a means of facilitating turning the mousse from the mold. Return the mold to the refrigerator to chill.

Grind through your finest meat grinder enough lean ham, with all fat and tendon removed, to yield a loosely packed cupful. Stir into it ½ cup of cold white sauce (béchamel) and ½ cup of the aspic. In another bowl whip stiff a cup of heavy cream (½ pint), and fold into it with a two-tined fork the ham mixture. Pour it into the chilled, aspic-coated mold, and proceed as with the other molded aspics, again using any leftover aspic for decoration. When turned out on its serving platter, the mousse should look like some Bavarian cream dessert, pinkish white, just glazed with the aspic with which you coated the mold. At its best this is a delicate dish, firm enough to slice well, a meat analogue of the mousse of chocolate of Menu 30. A mousse of chicken, preferably of clear white meat, can be made by the same procedure.

Two other variants of the basic procedure for beef aspic are well worth remembering. The first involves a sauce which ordinarily appears in the United States only in restaurants and clubs, and seldom there—hot-cold sauce, or, more properly, *chaud-froid.*

Chaud-froid: make a velvet sauce (see p. 153) of chicken consommé "with gelatin added," i.e., a consommé which when iced yields jellied chicken consommé. Soften 1 teaspoonful of unflavored crystalline gelatin in ¼ cup of white wine, and add it and ¼ cup of heavy cream to the velvet. Allow this sauce to cool but not to jell. Again this is a reversible process; should the sauce jell, you can bring it back to a liquid over a little heat. It is best manipulated when syrupy. It is a delicate sauce, and in classic cookery its flavor is often strengthened by the addition of a small quantity, say 2 tablespoonfuls, of the "essence" of some vegetable, i.e., of the water in which shredded mushroom stems or celery slices have been boiled long enough to yield most of their flavor; this water, drained from the vegetable, is then reduced by boiling to a really strong "essence."

The use of this sauce can be illustrated by one dish:

Breast of chicken chaud-froid: for two buy 2 breasts of chicken at a "chicken-in-pieces" shop. Remove the skin, and cutting with a sharp knife down from the breastbone, at the front along the "wishbone," pare off the white breast meat: it should come off in near-crescent-shaped pieces; trim them to regularize them in that shape. (You can make a chicken stock of the remains, but that is up to you. I usually do, if time allows, to provide the stock needed for the next stage, keeping the white meat moist by soaking it in cold water.) Poach the regularly shaped breasts in a baking dish in a 300° oven for thirty minutes in diluted chicken consommé (¾ cup of water, ¼ cup of consommé). When sufficiently cool, chill the breasts in the remainder of the diluted consommé in which they poached (again to keep them moist) in the refrigerator. When they are thoroughly chilled, have ready chaud-froid that is syrupy; dry them, and immerse them in it till they are thoroughly coated with it. Lift them from it with as much sauce as will cling to them and put them on a dish; spoon over each piece more of the syrupy sauce so that they are coated as thickly as possible with it. Return them to the refrigerator till the sauce has thoroughly jelled. With a spatula lift each piece from the dish and arrange them on the platter on which you will serve them. At this point you can decorate each piece in some appropriate way, traditionally with slices of truffles, or, if you have none handy, with neatly cut slices of black ripe olives. When arranged and decorated, they should be returned to the refrigerator on their platter till you wish to serve them. Again, in hot weather it is well to serve them over ice.

The other variant worth remembering is mayonnaise that clings, *mayonnaise collée:*

Mayonnaise collée: stir into mayonnaise (as much as you wish to use) half as much beef aspic cooled to be syrupy. Apply to chicken, lobster, or shrimp, just as the *chaud-froid* was applied to the breasts of chicken.

Finally you can similarly make a fish aspic, using *fumet de poisson* (see Menu 25) instead of a meat consommé, and adding a full white wine for the final flavoring instead of marsala. But I invariably find fish aspics just too fishy. Since they are very useful in keeping cold fish choice and moist, I have developed a simple jelly which I prefer for this purpose:

Aspic for fish: soften 2 teaspoonfuls of unflavored crystalline gelatin in ¼ cup of white wine. When it is pasty, melt it into 1 cup of white wine flavored with 1 teaspoonful of tarragon vinegar, and proceed as with meat aspic.

This jelly is particularly appropriate with cold salmon, sliced across the fish in slices known in French as *darnes:*

Darne of salmon, in jelly: for two, buy 2 inch-thick slices of salmon sliced across the fish. In a saucepan make what in French is called a "short stock," a court bouillon, but omitting the fish bones and fragments the classic recipe calls for (salmon is fishy enough in itself); simmer in 2 cups of water and 1 cup of white wine for thirty minutes 1 small grated onion, 5 stalks of parsley, ten grinds on the pepper grinder, ¼ teaspoonful of thyme, ¼ teaspoonful of marjoram. Lay the salmon slices in a baking dish, and straining off the seasonings, pour over them the clear court bouillon. Poach them in this broth in a 300° oven for thirty minutes and when sufficiently cool put them in the refrigerator in the broth (to keep them moist) till they are chilled. Drain and dry them. Put them on a plate and coat them as thickly as you can with syrupy aspic for fish, repeating the process to thicken the coating. Return to the refrigerator to allow the coating to jell. When it has, transfer them to the serving platter by lifting them gently on a spatula, and put them in the refrigerator until you wish to serve them. Any left-over aspic may be chopped with a spoon and used to decorate the platter. The jellied darnes may be decorated with slices of cucumber, and a cucumber salad (see p. 174) makes a fine accompaniment for this dish, particularly when fresh dill is in season.

While these procedures with aspic may sound complicated on first reading, in the long run they become one of the most enjoyable phases of cookery. They have the great advantage of being carried through well in advance of a meal. They deteriorate little, if any, under refrigeration during twelve hours or more. And they yield some of the handsomest dishes in all good cookery.

7. DESSERTS

For years I cherished the belief that there are few more satisfying desserts than cheese and fruit, and few that are more generally appropriate to a fine meal, particularly when the swelling years come on you. I tend still to prefer them. But the writing of the earlier version of this book was a forceful reminder that others, particularly those who have not yet to think of their caloric intake, prefer more variety than fruit and cheese seem to them to afford. Accordingly, I began to experiment with a broader range of desserts: some of them I had known from earlier times; some I discovered on this particular quest. But all of them have now been tested and retested in constant use, more for my guests than for myself, though I now have to acknowledge a certain hankering for many of them.

The range of those included even now may seem limited to devotees of pie, ice cream, and pudding. But recently, in browsing through the specimen menus included in *L'Art Culinaire Français* as typical of the best menu building, I was struck by the fact that the range of desserts represented there was almost precisely that of the pages that follow. Many of them are special ways of serving fruits.

Refreshed pineapple: this formerly expensive fruit is now quite reasonable in price, easy to handle, and with a little handling, particularly rewarding. Buy a pineapple that is ready to eat: your fruit man ought to be able to pick it out for you; his test of ripeness is both the feeling of the edible part and whether or not one of the center leaves at the top pulls out easily. With your chef's knife cut the pineapple crosswise into ½-inch slices: discard the top and bottom. Peel each slice around (slice in left hand, knife in right hand) deeply enough to remove the thorny skin and the pits; cut out the tough center in an even circle with your knife or an apple corer. Arrange the doughnut-shaped slices in the bowl in which you wish to serve them; sprinkle them with 2 to 3 tablespoonfuls of confectioners' sugar and pour over them ½ cup of some liqueur, traditionally, the clear white Swiss cherry brandy, kirsch, or, lacking it, a white curaçao, such as cointreau, or even the cooking liqueur suggested above (see p. 54): vodka flavored with orange or lemon peel. The liqueur may be added, as in French restaurants, just as the pineapple is served on each diner's plate; but this dessert seems to me to improve for sitting an hour or so in it.

Pineapple and strawberries: in the season when the two are available, buy both. With your kitchen scissors cut off most of the leaves on the pineapple, in effect trimming their core leaves to a point; if you happen to get a pineapple whose leaves are perfect and thus decorative, they can be left untrimmed. Lay the pineapple on its side and with your chef's knife cut down through it lengthwise, leaves and all, to divide it into halves. With your chef's knife cut out the center core from each half, most readily in a long, triangular wedge, and then cut the flesh of each half from the skin around the edge; finally, with vertical slices, cut the flesh thus loosened into ¼-inch wedges, so that the flesh can be served at the table with a spoon.

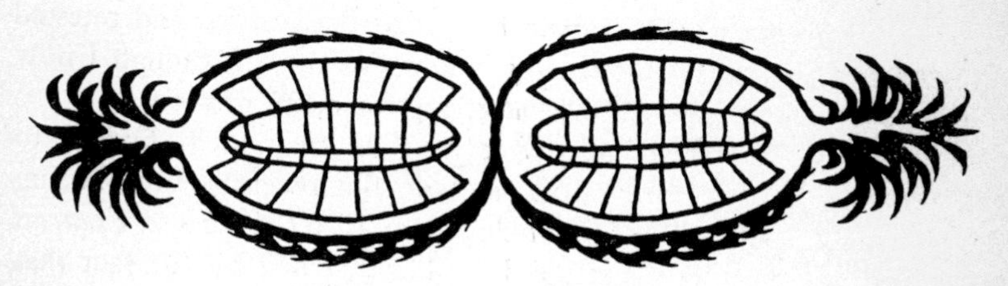

Cutting the pineapple

Wash and hull the strawberries. Put the pineapple halves bottom to bottom on a platter, and lay some of the strawberries in the space on each half from which you removed the core; arrange the rest of the berries around the pineapple halves on the platter. Sprinkle over both 2 to 3 tablespoonfuls of confectioners' sugar, and pour over the pineapple halves ½ cup of some liqueur, most appropriately those mentioned for Refreshed Pineapple, above.

Strawberries in (and with) white wine: it can be any white wine, but best a fine, really sweet, French sauterne. They are now to be found in the wine shops, often in half bottles, and at reasonable prices because they are too sweet for most tastes and uses, though perfect for this one. Recommended for this use are Château Yquem, or, better still, if you can find it, Rayne Vigneau. Wash and hull the strawberries; put them in the bowl in which you wish to serve them, and pour over them approximately a quarter of a half bottle of the wine; chill the rest, and drink it as you eat the berries.

Many fine fresh fruits are not impaired, but in fact are somewhat embellished, by what, surprisingly in English, is known as *stewing*. Their proper treatment is better described by the equivalent French term, *poaching*. For this treatment buy as many pears, peaches, apricots, or nectarines as you want, preferably a bit on the unripe side. Prepare them for stewing by removing their skins. Pears are peeled like apples with your slit-center paring knife, not round and round, but rather with long, lengthwise parings that leave a well-shaped product; if the stems remain, leave them on. Peaches, apricots, and nectarines are peeled like tomatoes, by brief immersion (ten seconds usually suffices) in briskly boiling water; after they cool thirty seconds their thin skins should readily come off under a knife's gentle persuasion, leaving the flesh unmarred. To stew such fruits in the French way, follow this procedure.

Stewed fruit: put to boil for ten minutes 1 quart of water, flavored with ½ cup of sugar and two inches of a vanilla bean, split so that the tiny seeds can be scraped into the water. When the fruit is peeled, reduce the heat under the water so that it is barely at a boil, and put in the fruit. Simmer for from five to ten minutes. The fruit may simply be served in this broth, with the vanilla bean removed. But the more elaborate version of this dessert, which figures in several subsequent desserts, calls for an alternative procedure from this point on. Remove the fruit from the broth and let it cool. Continue boiling the broth till it has reduced to a thick syrup no more than ½ cup in volume. At this point add some colored conserve: 2 to 3 tablespoonfuls of red apple jelly, strawberry marmalade, or the purée of apricots that can be bought in small tins as "baby food." Arrange the stewed fruit on a platter, and spoon over them, slowly, so that as much as possible will stick, this colored syrup. They will be handsomely glazed and colored by it. An admissible short cut for this recipe is to buy these same fruits canned, to reduce the juice in the can in the same way, and to flavor and color it in the same way.

One further step produces a still more striking fruit dessert:

Flamed fruit: stew the same fruits (pears, peaches, apricots, or nectarines) by the full procedure of the preceding recipe. Just before serving them, warm them and the platter on which you are serving them in a 200° oven for five minutes; at the same time warm briefly ¼ cup of brandy or some appropriate liqueur (kirsch, cointreau, or orange-peel-flavored vodka). Pour the liqueur over them, and light it with a match. Traditionally, it is lighted in the kitchen and the platter is brought in flaming; for greater safety, it can be lighted at the table, where the guests can watch the flaming liquid gently caramelizing the sauce on the fruits. This flaming is more dramatic if the light in the room is reduced.

Another classic dessert of this kind is

Jubilee cherries: wash a pound of fresh cherries and remove their stems and stones: the stones can be neatly removed with the loop of a wire hairpin, or with a little syringe-like gadget now available in kitchen shops that simply pushes them through. Stew them in a syrup made of 1 quart of water and ½ cup of sugar for ten minutes; remove the cherries with a perforated spoon and reduce the syrup by further boiling to the volume of 1 cup. Add ½ teaspoonful of arrowroot flour softened in ⅛ cup of white wine. Traditionally, Jubilee cherries are served in individual silver cups (*coupes*), but they can quite as well be served in a small silver bowl. They are finished by flaming them in ½ cup of some heated liqueur, most appropriately the liqueur derived from them, kirsch, or any other cherry brandy. To succeed with this flaming, since the cherries are cold, this liqueur must be well heated.

Another classic use of cherries as a dessert requires preparation weeks in advance; but cherries so prepared keep indefinitely.

Brandied cherries: when cherries are at their best and cheapest buy as many as you think you can use. Simply wash them well, leaving in the stones and carefully retaining any stems. Pack them tightly into pint preserving jars. Scatter over the cherries in each jar 1 teaspoonful or more if you prefer them sweeter, of confectioners' sugar. Fill each jar with an inexpensive vodka: the "brandy" called for in the French recipe is white *eau de vie*, essentially alcohol, which in the United States is best procured in unflavored vodka. Seal them tightly. Let the jars stand in a dark, cool place (e.g., a closet) for five weeks, turning them occasionally to help the sugar to dissolve. To serve, they may be simply poured out into a bowl, and, if you succeed in finding cherries with stems and in retaining them, eaten in the fingers by the stems. Remember that any of the juice that remains is essentially a cherry brandy and may be used as such, for example on pineapple or strawberries, or as the final flavoring in a Swiss fondue. You should be warned, however, that it is not strong enough, alcoholically, to flame well. A very special nondessert use of them is as a garnish for roast duck in the various styles bearing the name of Montmorency.

Another fruit that stews well and rewardingly is the kumquat, the tiny oranges that are now regularly on the market in the autumn.

Stewed kumquats: buy a basket of kumquats, remove the stems, wash well, and stew, without vanilla, for twenty minutes in a syrup made of 1 quart of water and ½ cup of sugar. Serve in their unreduced syrup.

Kumquats, so stewed, are very like an orange marmalade. It may be remarked at this point, therefore, that a neglected series of desserts resides in the fine marmalades now readily procurable, served, perhaps, with cottage cheese or its Italian counterpart, ricotta. Try, for example, with such a cheese, a ginger marmalade.

Baked apples become a dessert worthy of many a meal if done in the style known as

Baked apples à la bonne femme: with an apple corer, core 2 tart cooking apples; with your paring knife peel the skin around their tops down no more than an inch. Put them in a baking dish, put ½ cubic inch of butter in the hole left by coring, and sprinkle ½ teaspoonful of granulated sugar over each. Finally, sprinkle them with ¼ cup of white wine, and bake them for twenty minutes in a 350° oven. At the end of this time the butter, sugar, and wine will have run into the baking dish to form there a rich brown syrup. Remove the apples from the oven, and baste them with this syrup several times as they cool. Serve slightly warm, or cold, as you prefer.

As in the case of marmalades, not to be neglected are some of the comparable possibilities of apples: a fine applesauce, freshly made as in Menu 2, but slightly sweetened, goes as well with the cottage cheese; or one can now buy in jars spiced scarlet crabapples as fine as he could make himself, which provide a dessert in themselves, which may be flamed, and which, incidentally, provide a more brilliant accompaniment for the pork chops of Menu 2 than the applesauce there suggested.

With one more elaboration stewed fruits, including these spiced crabapples, become the crowning glory of a series of classic desserts. The elaboration, which they crown, is the French counterpart of rice pudding:

Rice in milk (riz au lait): for two, boil 1 cup of rice for five minutes in water, simply to blanch it. Meanwhile, warm in a saucepan with a removable handle 1 quart of milk, ⅔ cup of sugar, 1 cubic inch of butter, ¼ teaspoonful of salt, 2 inches from a vanilla bean, split lengthwise so that its tiny seeds may be scraped into the milk, and the finely grated peel of half a lemon. Drain the rice from its blanching water and pour it into the flavored milk. When it comes to a boil, remove the saucepan's handle and put it into a 350° oven for thirty minutes. By the end of this period the rice should be thoroughly cooked, but the mixture should still be soupy. While it is cooking, separate from their whites into a small bowl the yolks of 3 eggs; beat them till they turn a lighter yellow; dilute them with 1 tablespoonful of milk, and briefly beat again. At the end of thirty minutes remove the rice in milk from the oven, and on the kitchen bench blend into it with a two-tined fork the beaten egg yolks, which will quickly cook from the heat of the rice and milk and thicken the pudding. While it is still warm, pour the rice off onto the serving dish you intend to serve it on (preferably a round dish) into a mound corresponding in shape to the dish, and let it cool. If you are preparing rice in milk in advance, remember that it should be somehow covered and refrigerated, because of the susceptibility of only partly cooked egg yolks to contamination.

With this rice in milk as a basis you are ready for a series of dessert uses. Here one will suffice to suggest the series:

Apricots à la Condé: prepare rice in milk and mound it on a serving dish. Peel and stew apricots, in this instance cutting them in half after they are stewed and removing the stones. Some will be damaged in the process: return them to the reducing syrup, and when it is reduced force them and the syrup through the Foley Food Mill to provide the apricot sauce this dessert requires; serve it apart in a bowl. Arrange the half apricots, stone side down, on the mound of rice in milk. Scatter over it and them pieces of candied and colored fruit that you buy in a jar in the United States for making fruitcake.

For similar desserts, all of which are named in classic cookery, you can use stewed pears (with sweetened vanilla'd whipped cream, Imperial Pears), peaches, nectarines, and apples.

Always to be remembered for desserts are fine berries other than the strawberries already mentioned. At their best, they are served well washed simply by and for themselves, or, if you will, with fine sweet or sour cream. One dessert use of them, vastly superior to the fruit jellies, particularly those which come from flavored crystalline gelatin in envelopes, deserves special mention:

Rød Grød: this recipe I owe to a paragon among cooks, Mrs. Magda Rasmussen Abraham, on whose account I give it its Danish rather than its German name, *Rote Grütze*, red gruel. It is one recipe for which there are not precise directions, because it varies with its ingredients. It is made with at least two, possibly three, ingredients, chosen as the season allows from such as raspberries, blueberries, red currants, or cherries. The chosen ingredients are boiled in approximately 1 quart of water for thirty minutes and then puréed through the Foley Food Mill, but without attempting to force all the flesh through: what is wanted, primarily, is the juice they have yielded to the water. The juice is then returned to a saucepan over moderate heat, is sweetened to your taste, and is flavored in further boiling with 2 inches from a vanilla bean, split lengthwise and scraped to put into the broth its tiny seeds. After twenty minutes of moderate boiling the vanilla bean is removed, and the broth is thickened with arrowroot flour softened in cold water in the proportion of 5 tablespoonfuls to 1 quart of liquid. It is poured hot into the bowl in which you wish to serve it, and when sufficiently cool is refrigerated. Before serving, garnish its top with blanched, skinned, but otherwise raw almonds: i.e., shell almonds, boil them three minutes to loosen their inner skins, and pop the skins off between your fingers. Rød Grød is served with a pitcher of heavy cream, and any self-respecting Dane will eat a quart of it. It should not be so stiff as a jellied dessert, yet should not quite run on the plate. It is a dish for which precise directions are hardly possible, one you cannot ever fail with, and yet one you always think you can improve on a bit the next time you do it: these qualities are its charm for the cook.

Three fine desserts depend on the availability of chestnuts, whole or in purée (see p. 169).

Marrons glacés: bring to a boil a rich syrup of 2 cups of water and 1 cup of sugar flavored with 2 inches from a vanilla bean, split lengthwise so that the tiny seeds can be scraped into the syrup. Simmer in it for thirty minutes whole chestnuts. Cool and serve as a dessert in themselves. Or, adding a little brandy or rum to them while they cool, pour them over slices of the plain yellow cake known as poundcake, with sweetened whipped cream, to produce what, in New England, goes for Tipsy Parson.

Tête de Nègre: a variation of the classic recipe built around rice in milk. Finish an unseasoned chestnut purée by adding to it a little milk flavored with a vanilla bean (and its seeds) by simmering it a few minutes. Let the purée with the seasoned milk cook for twenty minutes in the top of a double boiler to season through and stiffen. When sufficiently stiff, mound it in a dome on a round serving platter and cover it with a chocolate sauce. Make the chocolate sauce as follows: In the top of a double boiler over hot water, melt 1 square of unsweetened chocolate (1 ounce) and add to it 1 cup of milk and ¼ cup of sugar; separate from their whites in a small bowl 2 egg yolks and beat till they are a lighter yellow; dilute them with 1 tablespoonful of milk and beat briefly again. Add the beaten yolks to the sweetened chocolaty milk in the double boiler top, and cook over hot water on moderate heat till it is a thick sauce. Pour it over the dome of chestnut purée on the serving plate, spreading it, if necessary, with a knife, like the frosting it is. Let it cool, and then with a teaspoon make two holes through the chocolate sauce into the purée for eyes, a curving opening below for the mouth, to justify the title of the dish. Serve with sweetened whipped cream.

Turinois: presumably named for the city. Again, finish a chestnut purée by adding to it a little milk flavored with a vanilla bean (and its seeds) by simmering it a few minutes. Let the purée and the flavored milk cook in the top of a double boiler for twenty minutes to season through and stiffen. During this cooking melt into it 2 1-ounce squares of unsweetened chocolate, ½ cup of sugar, and approximately one-fifth of its volume of butter. Line a baking pan, preferably a small bread pan, with aluminum foil, and pack this mixture into it hot. When it has cooled sufficiently, refrigerate to harden. Serve by turning it upside down out of the pan, removing the foil, and slicing in ½-inch slices like bread. Serve with Sauce Anglaise (soft custard).

Sauce Anglaise: in the top of a double boiler warm 1 cup of milk to which has been added ¼ cup of sugar and 2 inches from a vanilla bean, with its seeds scraped into the milk. Separate from their whites into a small bowl the yolks of two eggs; beat till they are a lighter yellow, dilute with 1 tablespoon of milk, and beat briefly again. Pour the beaten yolks into the flavored milk, heat over the hot water in the bottom of the double boiler over low heat until the sauce has thickened. If you wish it may be further seasoned with a tablespoonful of marsala or brandy.

For many readers this may seem to be a dessert to end all desserts, because of its richness. Actually, it is so delicious that a little goes a long way—and the rest keeps well under refrigeration for another day.

Having begun this book with eggs, the meals it suggests will conclude with desserts based essentially on eggs. Readers will surely have been asking what to do with all the egg whites that have been separated from their yolks in its pages. Occasionally I use them to clarify a meat stock; generally I throw them away. But there is one rewarding use of them which is a fine accompaniment for many desserts, even ice cream:

Meringues: the basic proportions for meringues are the whites of 4 eggs to ½ pound of confectioners' sugar into which has been stirred the seeds from 2 inches of vanilla bean. Beat the egg whites stiff and fold the sugar into them with a two-tined fork. Butter lightly a baking pan or sheet, and spoon the paste on it in mounds smaller than you wish the finished product to be. Theories of baking the meringues vary widely: some recipes call for a long, slow cooking in the lowest possible oven; the classic recipe is for a relatively quick cooking in a 400° oven, which yields a product crisp outside but creamy at its center. Accordingly, cooking times vary greatly. This is one dish on which it is best to experiment.

Returning to whole eggs, and disregarding many other desserts based on eggs, for example, the tricky sweet soufflés, one generally neglected dessert use of eggs deserves special treatment, now that you have learned to make a perfect omelet (see p. 162):

Sweet omelets: make an omelet seasoned with salt but substituting 1 teaspoonful of sugar for the pepper. Have the broiler heating, and a lightly buttered platter ready which will resist its heat briefly. Before folding the omelet, lay on the axis of the fold some conserve, e.g., apple jelly, strawberry marmalade; when it is folded, sprinkle its top with a tablespoonful of confectioners' sugar, and expose it briefly to the broiler's heat so that it will brown and the sugar will caramelize slightly. It may be served as is, or flamed with ⅛ cup of warmed rum, brandy, or a liqueur.

Crêpes Suzette remain for many Americans the *ne plus ultra* of desserts. Yet I suppose few Americans have eaten them really well made. All too often they are heavy and soggy in far too much sauce. They were best made, I am told, in the old Restaurant Foyot in Paris, and the tradition is maintained in a modest but excellent restaurant directed by one of Foyot's *maîtres d'hôtel* on the Ile St. Louis. There, as in this book, they come to the table relatively dry and on the point of being crisp. Furthermore, their preparation toward this norm allows their completion well in advance.

The recommended procedure is here divided into two stages, first that for preparing the French pancakes called for in Menu 20 and for other similar uses; second, the steps by which they are transformed into *Crêpes Suzette*.

French pancakes: the proportions for this batter are easy to remember: 3 beaten whole eggs, 1 cup of flour, 1 cup of milk to which is added 1 tablespoonful of oil, 1½ teaspoonfuls of salt or sugar, the former for such uses as the stuffed pancakes of Menu 20, the latter for pancakes for dessert. For two, two-thirds of this recipe is ample, i.e., 2 eggs, ⅔ cups of flour and milk, 2 teaspoonfuls of oil, 1 teaspoonful of salt or sugar. Beat the eggs in a bowl; add the flour, milk, oil, salt, or sugar, and beat again. Put 1 teaspoonful of vegetable fat in a frying pan and melt it over a brisk heat till the fat smokes. Pour enough of the batter into the pan to cover half its surface and by tilting it spread this amount over the entire surface: don't be troubled if it is so thin that little holes appear; these pancakes are supposed to be crêpey. When brown appears around the edges, slip under the pancake your broad spatula (pancake turner) and lift it from the pan; don't be alarmed when it will droop from the spatula; with a quick flip of your wrist turn it uncooked side down for brief cooking, and don't be distressed if it doesn't fall quite flat. After the briefest cooking on this second side, turn it out of the frying pan, second side up, on a paper towel on the kitchen shelf. Repeat the process, adding each time ½ teaspoonful of vegetable fat to keep the frying pan well greased. When the crêpes have cooled, you can easily handle them in arranging them for whatever purpose you have in mind: there is no real need to keep them hot.

Crêpes Suzette: for two, make crêpes from two-thirds of the basic recipe, sweetened. In a buttered frying pan with a heat-resistant or removable handle in which you are willing to bring them to the table arrange them folded lengthwise three times, with the folded ends down, across the pan, sprinkling along each a generous amount of prepared sugar: 1 cup of granulated sugar into which you have stirred the finely grated peel of an orange. Dot each pancake liberally with butter, and finally sprinkle over them the juice of the orange whose peel you used. When you sit down to dinner, put the pan, handle removed if it is not heat-resistant, into a 200° oven. Just before serving remove the pan from the oven, restoring its handle, and briefly heat it over moderate heat on the top of the stove. The crêpes should now be near crisp, the butter and the sugar should be blended together, and the entire dish should be relatively dry. Pour over it ¼ cup of some liqueur, warm it a bit more, light the liqueur, and carry the pan flaming to the table. Traditionally, the folded crêpes are served folded once again in the middle. An alternative is to do the flaming at the table, under the greedy eyes of your guests: this is easily arranged if you have some table heater—even a small electric plate. The classic recipe is supposed to call for flaming in ⅓ brandy, ⅓ Grand Marnier, and ⅓ curaçao or cointreau. I find that my orange-peel-flavored vodka serves quite as well.

Though a dessert may end a given meal, a good cook, as earlier remarked, is, among other things, one who during any meal and rising from it, thinks of going on to fresh conquests. Thus the two following sections are intended to suggest new fields of conquest by opening up two further ways of cooking—and throughout the bill of fare.

8. PÂTE À CHOUX

The preceding thirty menus, and what is proposed in this à la carte section, call for no pastry, with the single exception of Quiche Lorraine, for which ordinary piecrust will serve. For years I eschewed pastry making in the belief that it was difficult and fattening. It may be the latter, though not necessarily if eaten in moderation; but it need not be difficult. To carry other cooks into new terrain, this section will describe how one basic ingredient of pastry making is made, and what can be done with it: *pâte à choux*, so called because it is the paste from which are made what in French are called *petits choux*, in English, cream puffs.

In *haute cuisine* an apprentice learns to make it early in his training, and simple enough it is to make and to keep in the refrigerator for a few days at least.

Pâte à choux: melt in a saucepan in 1 cup of water 5 cubic inches of butter, adding ½ teaspoonful of salt. When the butter is melted and the water is boiling, sift in 1 cup of flour, stirring it with a wooden spoon, as it quickly becomes a heavy paste. Continue to cook this paste over a gentle flame (thoroughly to cook the flour) for as much as ten minutes, kneading it with the spoon, which as it cooks will go in and out of it cleanly. While it is cooking (between kneadings) beat well 4 whole eggs. After ten minutes' cooking remove the pan from the stove, and stir in the beaten eggs a little at a time (say in four portions), simply because they will be absorbed only a little at a time. When they are absorbed, the paste is ready, either for immediate use, or, refrigerated, for later uses.

In its different uses this paste figures in almost every section of the bill of fare. Its uses as an hors d'oeuvre are among the most distinctive.

Gougère Bourguignonne: served as a first course, particularly when tasting a fine, red burgundy. Make the standard paste with two variations: less butter, 3 cubic inches, while beating in the eggs, add also 1 cupful of Swiss cheese in ¼-inch cubes. Spoon out the mixture into a rough ring on a buttered pastry sheet or baking pan, working the spoonfuls together with your fingers. Bake approximately twenty minutes, or until brown and puffy, with the cheese cubes standing out in it, in a 400° oven. Serve warm, rather than hot, by cutting out slices of the ring. Since half this quantity makes a *gougère* sufficient for three to four persons, reserve the rest of the paste for use another day as:

Ramequins: the same paste, laid out in teaspoonful quantities on a buttered baking tin, baked for the same time in a 400° oven, to produce, except for the protuberant cubes of cheese, what look like cream puffs. They can be passed during cocktails, served as an hors d'oeuvre at the table, or even as a cheese dessert.

Even a small quantity of the standard paste will provide a garnish for soups, if similarly baked, naturally for a somewhat shorter time, in ¼-teaspoonful dots on a buttered sheet.

Two instances of how the standard paste figures as an ingredient in the main course will suffice. The first is another and more delicate French version of the Gnocchi, Roman style, p. 165.

Gnocchi à la Parisienne: boil and purée through the Foley Food Mill 1 small potato, mixing into the purée an approximately equal quantity of grated spaghetti cheese. This mixture should be added to approximately five times as much *pâte à choux.* Fill a saucepan with cold water, and squeeze into it from a pastry bag little cylinders, ½ inch in diameter, about 2 inches long; by laying your long knife across the pan they can easily be cut off at that length. Slowly bring the water to a boil, and just as it begins to boil, lift out the gnocchi, which, as they soufflée, will have risen to the top. Lay them in a buttered baking dish, sprinkle spaghetti cheese over them, dot with butter, and bake till light brown. They are good enough in this form, although the classic recipe calls for covering them with white sauce to which has been added ¼ cup of cream.

Potatoes Dauphine: boil and purée through the Foley Food Mill 3 medium-sized potatoes; season with salt, pepper, and a little nutmeg; to be sure the purée is completely dry, stir in the seasonings over a gentle heat. Off the fire, stir in the beaten yolks of 2 eggs and approximately a quarter (by volume) of *pâte à choux.* Pour this mixture onto a buttered dish and chill in the refrigerator. When it is cold, roll it, 1 tablespoonful at a time, into cylinders the size of a wine-bottle cork. Roll them in turn, first in flour, second in beaten egg, and last in bread crumbs. Fried in deep fat (see the following section), they present potatoes in probably their most delectable form.

In desserts, *pâte à choux* in only slightly different form, i.e., sweetened, figures in so many ways that I will cite only two. If it is intended for desserts, 1 tablespoonful of sugar is added to the water in which the butter is melted at the outset. But the sugar may be added later, when the beaten eggs are being stirred in; and I often divide a batch at this stage, stirring sugar into one, leaving the other merely salted, e.g., for ramequins. Sweetened and baked on a buttered baking sheet or pan it yields:

Eclairs, Cream Puffs, or Profiteroles, differentiated by their shapes. Each can be shaped through a pastry bag, but a teaspoon and the fingers serve almost as well: éclairs, before baking and rising, should be approximately ½ inch in diameter and 3 inches long; cream puffs, approximately 2 inches in diameter; profiteroles, somewhat smaller. Traditionally, éclairs are garnished lengthwise with Sauce Anglaise (see Desserts, p. 191) either plain or chocolate-flavored (and remember that since an egg sauce like this is an ideal medium for ptomaine poisonings, when once filled with it they should be eaten at once or refrigerated). In American usage cream puffs or profiteroles are most congenial when broken open horizontally, and filled with a spoonful of ice cream. They, too, may be served, so filled, with Sauce Anglaise, either plain or chocolate-flavored.

9. DEEP-FAT FRYING

In compiling this book I have been handicapped by a decision, I hope mistaken, that many of its readers would turn back from deep-fat frying. Certainly, many inexperienced cooks regard it as a procedure that is difficult and dangerous. Properly handled, it need be neither. And it opens up so many possibilties of good cooking and good eating that it ought at least to be tried. Finally, perhaps more than any other way of cooking, it can be accurately managed.

To minimize the dangers (which are more imagined than real), have the following equipment and observe the following rules.

For *equipment* buy (1) a special deep-frying pan equipped with a basket and a proper support for the basket when it is out of the fat (I prefer a sheet-iron pan with an upright at the back on which the basket sits); (2) a deep-fat thermometer with a clip to hold it on the pan's side.

For *safety*, (1) in general, never leave the kitchen when fat is heating on the stove; (2) never allow its temperature to exceed 400°–incidentally, higher temperatures will brown and spoil your fat; (3) never fry except in the basket with your hand on its handle–fires from fat almost always occur from its boiling over when some moist ingredient makes it "boil"; if the ingredient is in the basket you can immediately stop the "boiling" by lifting it entirely or partly out of the fat; (4) handle hot, liquid fat with extreme care–evidently it burns badly if you spill it on your feet, to say nothing of the mess on the kitchen floor; (5) to minimize further all these risks, never have your frying pan more than half full of fat at most–this may mean frying smaller quantities in any given batch, but that is usually preferable, in any case.

After thirty years of experimentation I have come to the conclusion that peanut oil is the best frying fat. It is readily procurable, cheap, never hardens, and yields what now seems to me the best product. In using, as I did for years, vegetable and meat fats that harden when cold, I fell into the sloppy habit of simply leaving them in the frying pan, covered, to be sure, between using. A fat that does not solidify deserves better treatment, i.e., being poured off into

Ball jars through a strainer between uses. At any rate, after thirty years of error I now unreservedly recommend peanut oil to prospective deep-fat fryers.

You will readily convince yourself if you once make French-fried potatoes in it by the following procedure:

For two, peel two medium-sized potatoes; slice them lengthwise in ⅜-inch slices, and the slices again into ⅜-inch strips; the edge pieces may be retained as well. Set them to dry in paper towels.

On quick heat bring peanut oil (pan not more than half full) to 250°. Put the thoroughly dried potatoes in the frying basket and lower them gradually into the fat; at this temperature they will not quickly boil up; but stand with your hand on the basket's handle ready to lift them out if they should boil abnormally. Let them bubble till they are soft but not gilded, usually (potatoes vary) for about five minutes.

Turn off the heat and let the potatoes cool in the basket for ten minutes. Or, better still, if you can prepare them well in advance, pour them out on a paper towel in a pan and refrigerate them till just before you want to serve them.

Ten minutes before you wish to serve them, start the fat again and bring it to 300°. Replace the potatoes in the basket and fry them in the 300° fat till they are golden but not brown. In a matter of minutes they should be finished, hardly more than three minutes; let them drain briefly in the basket, and then further on a paper towel. Salt and serve: they should be mealy inside and crystalline-crisp on the outside. Try them with the steak of Menu 12, instead of the baked potatoes there prescribed, because I was afraid you wouldn't!

It is only fair to say that I arrived at my clarification on deep-fat frying through eating the potatoes of Mme. Jacques Havet, pharmacist, vineyard proprietor, gourmet, cook, and a Bordelaise, in Paris; hers could not be better, even if they had not been served at a luncheon graced by four wines from her vineyard!

A further advantage of peanut oil is that, easily stored in and pourable from bottles, you can keep two batches of fat going, the first, fresh and clean for frying that demands fat fresh and clean, the second for frying that does not. In the examples of what you can do by this procedure, the fats required will be indicated in this way: (1) *fresh and clean;* (2) *older.* To be sure, there comes a point which you will quickly recognize when an *older* fat is too old: however much you strain it, it will have turned brownish and accumulated too many assorted flavors; at this point it should be put out to pasture, down the drain, and well flushed down with the hottest water the faucet will provide—and replaced by the fat that was *fresh and clean*, which in turn is replaced by a new bottle. Obviously, between usings the frying pan, basket, and fat thermometer should be thoroughly washed *and dried:* dangerous spattering of hot fat can result if there is any water on these utensils; and it won't occur till the fat gets really hot. Be sure, then, to have them thoroughly devoid of any water before using.

Deep-fat frying makes possible the inclusion of new dishes to the menu in every section save soups and salads. A few of its possibilities will be described in the order of the classic bill of fare.

For hors d'oeuvres deep-fat frying offers many possibilities, as, for example, small croquettes of various meats (see below, p. 202). Two related possibilities are worth special mention:

Pigs in blankets: buy a dozen (more or less according to your needs) shelled oysters. Cut a long strip of bacon into pieces long enough to encircle the oysters. Dry the oysters on paper towels. (If you like oyster juice, drink it in the process.) Wrap each oyster in its piece of bacon and fix it by sticking a wooden toothpick through the oyster and the bacon. Fry the bacon and the oysters in 350° fat until the bacon is brown. Use older fat that is near going to pasture.

Olives in blankets: precisely the same procedure except that you substitute large stuffed olives for the oysters.

Surprising as this may seem, true fried eggs are fried in deep fat; says *L'Art Culinaire Français*, "The fried eggs of which so much use is made in breakfast in England and America are really 'eggs on the stove.' In these countries, the fried egg, in its proper form, is for all practical purposes, unknown." In their proper form:

Fried eggs: are broken out on a plate or saucer, are gently slid into deep fat at 350°, are stirred therein with a wooden spoon so that the white fries in a tight ball around the yolk (a wooden spoon, because the whites will stick to a metal spoon in the hot fat), and are cooked till the fat is slightly brown and crisp. Use fat that is fresh and clean.

For fish, deep-fat frying has in general dual possibilities, with respect to the coating the fish is given before frying. The first coating is by what is usually referred to in English as "breading" them, and it is applicable to scallops, shrimp, oysters, clams, sole, and "fish sticks," usually made of clear sticks of haddock.

To "bread" fish: soak the fish in question in milk. Wet with the milk, roll it in flour on a piece of waxed paper. Beat 1 (or more) whole egg, and spread bread crumbs on another piece of waxed paper. With your left hand immerse the floured pieces in the egg and lay them on the bread crumbs; with your uneggy right hand roll them in the bread crumbs till the eggy surface of the fish will absorb no more. Put them in the frying basket (or if you are preparing them for later use, in the refrigerator), and fry in 350° fat until they are golden brown. Use older fat that is near pasture, because the loose bread crumbs and fishy flavor will help to send it on its way.

The second coating for these same fish is what is known in English as "batter"; it is vastly inferior to its French counterpart, *pâte à frire*, which produces those "soufléed shrimps," for example, that you may have had in France.

Frying paste: mix into 1 cup of flour 1 tablespoonful of oil, 1 teaspoonful of salt, and ½ cup of water as hot as it comes from the faucet; stir the mixture into a paste and let it sit for an hour. When you are ready to use it, separate an egg, and beat the white till it is stiff; pour on it the paste and with a two-tined fork fold (do not stir) the egg white into it. Dip into this frothy mixture whatever is to be fried, and fry it in 350° fat by dropping it in, piece by piece, with the frying basket already in the fat, so that you can lift out the pieces when they have puffed and turned golden brown. Use fat that is fresh and clean.

Such frying produces excellent results with the same sea foods mentioned as candidates for breading, except for scallops, which, yielding liquid with heat, do better with the other coating.

Perhaps the prime candidate for such treatment is:

Fried Onion Rings: buy one or more large onions, a full three inches in diameter, and slice them crosswise into ½-inch slices. Carefully break out from each slice the larger rings, setting aside the rest to be kept in the refrigerator for some other use. With the two-tined fork stir these rings into *pâte à frire*, till they are thoroughly coated with it. In the frying pan with the basket in it to facilitate removing and draining them, fry these coated rings, four or five at a time, lifting them into the fat from the paste with the two-tined fork with as much paste clinging to them as you can retain. It will puff quickly in 350° fat to yield rings better than most. Lift the fried rings from the fat in the basket and let them drain there as the fat, cooled a bit by cooking them, rises again to 350°. Pour them off on paper towels on the platter on which you will serve them and keep in a warm place as you repeat the process enough times to produce as many rings as you want. Obviously, this is last-minute cookery, but well worth the trouble.

For main courses, deep-fat frying offers many possibilities. First and foremost are croquettes, usually made from ground leftover meats worked into a paste; in the case of white meats, with cold white sauce (béchamel); in the case of other meats, with cold, clear brown sauce. Such croquette pastes may further be garnished with small pieces of mushrooms, or with duxelles.

Croquettes: make a paste of whatever ground meat you wish to utilize (ground or diced chicken, turkey, lamb, ham, tongue) and the appropriate cold sauce—white sauce or clear brown sauce. Put flour on a piece of waxed paper; roll the paste into a cylinder the size of a French wine-bottle cork (approximately 3 inches long and 1 inch in diameter) and roll the cylinders in the flour. Beat a whole egg and finish them with the remaining stages of "breading." Fry them in the basket in 350° fat. Use older fat.

For vegetables, potatoes are the principal candidates for deep-fat frying. Two other varieties which are intended to be crisp, rather than crisp outside and mealy inside, call for somewhat different treatment.

Potato chips: peel and slice as many potatoes as you need, and slice them as thin as you can in rounds across the potatoes: in this it is advantageous to use a special slicer which you can procure in better kitchen shops; it serves other purposes as well—as, for example, slicing cucumbers. Soak the slices in cold water till they are crisp. Just before frying dry them in paper towels, and slide them individually into 350° fat, a handful at a time—i.e., take a handful, and with your two hands peel them into the fat one at a time, so that in the fat they will not stick together. Stir them in the fat with a two-tined fork. Cook them in one stage, until they just begin to turn golden brown; lift them out in the basket, where they will turn slightly browner, while the fat is coming back to 350° for the next batch. Potato chips need not be fried just before serving; they can be kept warm, or be briefly warmed in a 300° oven when you come to serve them. Use fat that is fresh and clean.

Potato straws: follow the procedure for potato chips, except that the potatoes are cut into slivers 2 to 3 inches long and less than ¼-inch square. An easy way to cut them for this use is to grate them through a medium grater. Crisp all through, they, too, need not be fried just before serving.

When you can so readily buy potato chips, making them at home may seem a work of supererogation. But guests who eat homemade chips for the first time tend to act as if they had never before known what potato chips could be like.

One other vegetable is an admirable and neglected candidate for deep-fat treatment:

Fried Eggplant: cut an eggplant crosswise in ½-inch slices; pare off the skin from each slice, and cut it crosswise into pieces approximately ½-inch square, i.e., the shape of potatoes for deep-fat frying. Put these slices on a platter and scatter over them 1 teaspoonful of salt, working it into them with your fingers. Let the eggplant sit for at least fifteen minutes: the salt will make it yield its extra water, which should be poured off. Spread ½ cup of flour on a piece of waxed paper and roll the eggplant pieces in it till they are well covered with it: wet as they will be, it will stick to them. Lay approximately half of them in the frying basket, give it a shake to shake off any extra flour, and fry the pieces in 350° fat until they are golden but not brown. Let them drain as the fat returns to 350°, pour them off on paper towels on the platter on which you will serve them, and keep them in a warm place while you repeat the process to fry the remaining pieces. This, again, is rewarding, but last-minute cookery.

I had always been fond of a traditional American dish, but never succeeded in making it to my satisfaction until I happened on a French version of it in the section of *L'Art Culinaire Français* devoted to American dishes:

Corn fritters: for two, separate an egg, and beat the yolk in one bowl, reserving the white in another for later use; add to the beaten yolk ⅓ cup of flour, ½ teaspoonful of salt, ½ teaspoonful of baking powder, a generous dash of paprika, and ½ cup of canned corn, cream style, with its liquid; mix these ingredients well. Beat stiff in the other bowl the white of the egg and pour on to it the mixture from the first bowl, blending it (not stirring it) into the beaten egg white. With the basket in the fat and the fat at 350°, put this now fluffy paste, 1 heaping tablespoonful at a time, into the fat and fry till it puffs more and turns a golden brown. Traditionally, these fritters are served with maple syrup. Use a fat that is fresh and clean.

This last dish approaches the dessert uses of deep-fat frying. It is largely based on the *pâte à frire* for which the recipe was given above, p. 201, except that it is not salted, but is given instead 1 teaspoonful of sugar and 1 teaspoonful of some flavoring before the egg whites are blended in, e.g., 1 teaspoonful of brandy or some liqueur, or of lemon or orange juice, or a small amount, approximately 1 teaspoonful, of grated lemon or orange peel. Inch-long pieces of banana, cut crosswise, and dipped in this paste when fried at 350°, yield delectable "banana fritters," or, as the French say, *beignets*. One other example will serve.

Apple fritters: core and pare as many apples as you want to use; cut them crosswise into ½-inch doughnut-like slices; sprinkle them liberally with sugar and then with rum or some liqueur. Let them soak up its flavor for as much as an hour, coat them in *pâte à frire* and fry them in 350° fat, dropping them one by one into the basket that is already in the fat. Serve them with a sprinkling of powdered sugar. Use fat that is fresh and clean.

Finally, this way of cooking combines with your acquired ability to prepare *pâte à choux* (see p. 195) to produce a similar dessert, known formally as *Beignets souflés*, more popularly as *Pets de nonnes* (for the explanation of which you are referred to any good French dictionary):

Beignets souflés: make a *pâte à choux* with 3 rather than 5 cubic inches of butter. As rapidly as possible drop teaspoonfuls of this mixture into fat at 300°, with the frying basket in it, in batches of ten or so at a time—as rapidly as possible, so that they cook evenly in batches. On full heat allow the fat to rise toward 350° and so the beignets to puff with the rising heat. Remove in the basket, drain there while you let the fat fall in temperature for the next batch, if there is to be one. Serve with powdered sugar sprinkled over them and more in a separate bowl. Use fat that is fresh and clean.

A rapid review of the foregoing pages will show you that this new method of cooking has opened up to you some twenty-five additional dishes. With them perhaps this book has led you far enough for the present into good eating, and so may gracefully come to an

END

INDEX

The index that follows is designed for users rather than for readers of this book. It therefore relates to (1) dishes it tells you how to cook and (2) procedures you will use in cooking them. For convenience, it lists dishes under their principal ingredients and under their common name (*e.g., Eggs, scrambled,* and *Scrambled eggs*).